500

stir-fry dishes

500

stir-fry dishes

the only compendium of stir-fry dishes you'll ever need

Michelle Keogh

SELLERS
PUBLISHING

A Quintet Book

Published by Sellers Publishing, Inc.
161 John Roberts Road, South Portland, Maine 04106
Visit our Web site: www.sellerspublishing.com
E-mail: rsp@rsvp.com

ISBN: 978-1-4162-4607-7
Library of Congress Control Number: 2016944809
QTT.FHSD

This book was conceived, designed and produced by
Quintet Publishing Limited
Ovest House
58 West Street
Brighton
BN1 2RA

Food Stylist: Jenny Brown
Photographer: Ian Garlick
Designer: Rod Teasdale
Art Director: Michael Charles
Project Editors: Julie Brooke, Leah Feltham
Editorial Director: Emma Bastow
Publisher: Mark Searle

10 9 8 7 6 5 4 3 2 1

Printed in China by 1010 Printing International Ltd.

contents

introduction

Stir-frying is an easy way to make a meal. Like the best one-pot cooking, all of the ingredients are cooked in the same pan. The method uses a small amount of very hot oil, and the heat cooks everything quickly, saving time, and retaining nutrients. All the preparation can be done ahead (including cooking the rice or noodles), which means you can get a meal to the table in just five to seven minutes — perfect when you are short on time but want to serve a healthy and delicious dish. What's more, this method of cooking is fun and easy to learn.

If you are new to stir-frying, see the section in this book about choosing and using a wok and the utensils you need to create authentic stir-fries. The Glossary (see page 280) describes the specialty ingredients used, but the beauty of stir-frying is that you can substitute foods and still make an authentic meal. For example, if you don't enjoy eating hot, bird's eye chiles, use long ones with a milder flavor; use ginger if you can't find galangal; or green beans rather than snow peas.

woks

The wok is one of the most common cooking utensils in China, because it has such a wide range of uses. It can be used for pan-frying, steaming, deep-frying, boiling, braising, poaching, searing, stewing, smoking, roasting and, of course, stir-frying. It's most recognizable feature is its shape — an inverse dome with a rounded bottom. Sometimes, woks have a flat bottom, similar to a deep skillet. This is generally so they can be used on an electric stove, because a round-bottomed wok doesn't have enough contact with the element to heat properly.

A wok with a round bottom allows the food to move around easily, because there are no corners for it to get caught in, and movement is the key to stir-frying. If food sits too long it may burn. Round-bottomed woks work best on gas burners, and some stoves have a burner just for woks with a larger burner and a trivet to hold the wok.

Woks are usually made of cast iron or carbon steel, but you can also find woks with a nonstick coating, or made from stainless steel or aluminum.

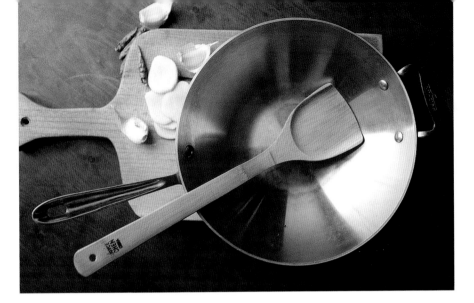

A flat-bottomed wok is essential for electric stoves. A wok spatula helps to stir the ingredients.

Each type of wok has its pros and cons, so be sure to learn about the durability, weight, consistency of heat, and time it takes for a wok to heat up or cool down when considering which style is best for your needs. Different types of woks are better suited to various stovetops, heat sources, and ventilation situations as well.

While a wok will give you the best results with your stir-fry, it is possible to stir-fry without a wok. A large, heavy-based (preferably stainless steel) skillet with slanted sides can be used to make a stir-fry. The sides of a skillet aren't as high as those on a wok, so you do lose some cooking area, but if you take care not to overload the pan this shouldn't present too much of a problem. Keeping the skillet in constant contact with the heat will also ensure you don't lose too much heat while cooking.

wok seasoning & maintenance

Seasoning your wok entails creating a layer of fat and oil on the surface that prevents food from sticking during cooking and stops rust from forming when the pan is not in use. All seasoning should be performed with great care, because there is a risk of burns to your skin and fire caused by the high temperatures and oil. If the wok starts to smoke furiously, remove it from the heat as it is in danger of catching fire.

Carbon steel and raw cast iron woks are often coated in a thin film of lacquer or wax to prevent them from rusting in transit. This must be removed before using the wok. Scour the pan in hot soapy water until all traces of the coating are gone, or burn it off using a high heat in a well ventilated area, preferably outside. Let the wok cool.

To season your wok, place it on the stovetop over a high heat until it is hot. Put in 2 or 3 tablespoons of canola or sunflower oil and move the wok back and forth to cover the inside surface with oil, taking care that it doesn't catch fire. When the inside surface has darkened, remove the wok from the heat and let it cool. Avoid steaming, poaching, and boiling in a newly seasoned wok, because this will upset the seasoning. For the same reason, avoid stir-frying acidic foods such as vinegar, lemons, and tomatoes until the wok has built up a good patina of seasoning.

Also avoid scrubbing your seasoned wok with dish detergent. To clean it, wipe it out using a sponge and hot water and place it over a low heat to dry, then rub the surface with lightly oiled paper towels. If there are hard-to-remove foods stuck to the surface, soak it in hot water for 5 to 10 minutes to loosen the food, then wipe out. Once the wok is clean and cool, store it in a dry, airy place, such as a cupboard. If it's not stored properly, the oil coating can turn rancid.

utensils

A wok ring can be used to create the high temperatures required for stir-frying. This ring of metal sits over the burner or electric element of a stove to direct and increase the heat. Choose one that fits your burners when the pan support has been removed.

The seasoned surface of this round-bottomed wok will prevent food from sticking while it cooks.

The only other special tool you should have when stir-frying is a wok spatula. This long-handled, spade-shaped scoop is shaped to fit the sides of a wok and is perfect for keeping the food moving around.

stir-fry preparation

Once you heat your wok to begin cooking, everything happens very quickly. Therefore, it is critical that all your ingredients are prepared, your utensils are ready and next to your wok, and your serving plates are waiting. If you are serving your stir-fry with a starch, such as rice or noodles, have this cooking before you begin so that it is ready once your stir-fry is cooked.

Seasonings, such as garlic, ginger, and chile, should be peeled and prepared according to your recipe's instruction.

Slice meat, poultry, and fish into evenly sized strips for even cooking and pat it dry using paper towels. Choose meats that will cook quickly and remain tender, such as beef fillet, pork fillet, or chicken breast.

Wash, peel, and slice vegetables: Harder vegetables, such as carrots and peppers, should be cut into thin strips to shorten

their cooking time. Thinly slicing other vegetables is preferable to cutting them into chunks. Leafy greens can be left whole or cut into smaller pieces, because they will wilt and cook quickly either way. Thick stems should be sliced.

All sauces and thickeners should be pre-measured and pre-mixed if necessary. If you are including noodles or rice in the stir-fry, have them cooked, drained, and ready to add before you start.

Placing each prepared ingredient onto a cutting board or into individual dishes in the order they will be added to the wok is helpful.

how to stir-fry

Once all the ingredients are ready to go, place the wok over high heat and heat it until a small drop of water evaporates in a second or two. Add the oil by pouring it in around the sides of the wok, and then add any aromatics or seasonings. Toss these quickly until they are fragrant, then quickly add any meat or tofu. Cook these for a few minutes, tossing every minute or so, until they are opaque, but not cooked through.

Woks are available in several different styles and shapes, including this one with two loop handles.

Once the meat or protein is partially cooked, it's time to add any firm vegetables. Add leafy vegetables such as bok choy, spinach, and cabbage toward the end, since they take less time to cook. Bean sprouts, noodles, and rice are also added toward the end of cooking, mostly just to heat them through and combine with the rest of the cooked ingredients.

Throughout the stir-fry process, keep moving the ingredients from the sides to the center of the wok so they cook evenly.

Add any sauce and thickeners by pouring them in around the edges so they don't cool the wok too much. Toss them to heat through and coat the other ingredients, then add fresh herbs just before serving.

If you are concerned about certain ingredients over-cooking, you can remove them from the wok to a warm plate using the wok spatula, continue to cook the other ingredients, then return them to the wok toward the end to quickly reheat. This can also be a good idea if you have trouble keeping the wok hot enough, since having fewer ingredients in the wok at once will help prevent heat loss.

rice

Most stir-fries are served alongside rice, or with rice as a main component of the dish. There are several ways to prepare rice, so choose a method that matches your time and equipment. Steamed, absorption, and boiled rice are cooked on the stove. You can also cook rice in a standard oven, in a microwave, or in a rice cooker. Jasmine, basmati, and other long-grain rice varieties are recommended with stir-fries. Check the package for rice to water ratios and cooking times, and plan ahead so your cooked rice is ready and waiting for your finished stir-fry.

flavored rice

When preparing rice, you can easily add some flavor by adding a little salt and a few aromatics to complement your main dish. Add 1/2 to 1 teaspoon of salt along with an ingredient to suit your stir-fry. Try one of these: a couple of slices of fresh ginger, a bruised stem of lemongrass, a couple of

Kaffir lime leaves, a couple of star anise, a finely sliced chile, a teaspoon of cumin seeds, a couple of whole garlic cloves. Adding 1/4 to 1/2 cup of fresh, chopped herbs to cooked rice when fluffing it will add extra flavor and a decorative touch.

coconut rice

Coconut rice makes a rich, indulgent accompaniment to your favorite dishes. Prepared here using a stove absorption method, it could easily be prepared in a rice cooker, or even in the microwave.

2 cups long-grain rice
1 1/2 cups coconut milk
1 1/2 cups water
1-in. (2.5-cm.) piece of fresh ginger
1/2 tsp. salt

- Put the rice into a strainer and run it under cold water until the water runs clear. Allow it to drain.
- Transfer the rice to a heavy saucepan and add the water and coconut milk. Bruise the ginger by pounding it lightly in a mortar and pestle, then add it to

Rice is the perfect accompaniment to a stir-fry. Add extra flavor by stirring through chopped herbs.

the pan with the salt. Shake the pan gently from side to side to level out the rice. Cover the saucepan with a tight-fitting lid or aluminum foil and place over high heat.

- Bring the rice to a boil and immediately reduce the heat to low. Allow the rice to cook, without lifting the lid, for about 12 minutes, or until all the water has been absorbed.

- Remove the saucepan from the heat and allow the rice to sit, without removing the lid, for 5 minutes. Remove the lid and use a fork to gently fluff the rice to separate the grains. Remove the ginger before serving.

chicken, duck & turkey

Poultry has been farmed throughout Asia for centuries, and generally most parts of the bird are used in some way. Stir-frying is a fantastic way to quickly cook the more tender cuts of chicken, duck, and turkey, or a way to use up leftovers from a roasted or grilled bird.

chili paste & chicken (pad phet)

see variations page 46

Making chili or curry pastes may seem daunting, but they're actually very simple to prepare. Traditionally, a mortar and pestle would be used to grind the ingredients, but this could just as easily be done in a food processor. Serve this dish with rice.

4–6 red bird's eye chiles, chopped
4 cloves garlic, peeled
1/2 oz. fresh ginger, chopped
2 tsp. coconut palm sugar or brown sugar
1/2 tsp. salt
1 small bunch fresh Thai basil, chopped
   (see Glossary, page 280)
1 tbsp. white vinegar

2 tbsp. peanut or vegetable oil
1 lb. chicken fillet, cut into bite-size pieces
1/2 small cauliflower, cut into bite-size florets
1/4 cup water
6 baby bok choy, quartered
8 oz. mung bean sprouts
fish sauce, to taste

Put the chiles, garlic, fresh ginger, sugar, salt, and half the Thai basil into a mortar and pestle. Pound to a rough paste before adding the vinegar, then pound again until combined.

Heat a wok until a drop of water evaporates in a second or two. Add the oil and chicken and stir-fry for 2 to 3 minutes, until partly cooked. Add the cauliflower and toss for another 1 to 2 minutes. Add the chili paste to the wok, stir-frying quickly until fragrant, then add the water, bok choy, and bean sprouts. Stir-fry for 1 to 2 minutes, until the bok choy begins to wilt and the chicken is cooked. Season with fish sauce, to taste. Sprinkle with the remaining Thai basil.

Serves 4

hoisin duck with spinach

see variations page 47

This is the perfect recipe for using up leftover cooked meat. Add it to the stir-fry later, because it only needs to heat through before serving. Sweet, salty, and spicy, hoisin sauce is a Chinese condiment that can be used for stir-frying or as a dip. This dish is delicious with noodles or rice.

2 tbsp. peanut or vegetable oil
2 cloves garlic, peeled and finely chopped
1/2 oz. fresh ginger, finely chopped
4 scallions, cut into bite-size pieces
1/2 large roast duck, flesh finely sliced

2 tbsp. light soy sauce
1/2 cup hoisin sauce
1 tbsp. rice wine
8 oz. baby spinach
8 oz. mung bean sprouts

Heat a wok until a drop of water evaporates in a second or two. Add the oil, garlic, ginger, and scallions, and stir-fry until fragrant and golden.

Add the duck and toss for 1 minute before adding the soy sauce, hoisin sauce, rice wine, spinach, and bean sprouts. Stir-fry until the spinach has wilted and the duck is heated through.

Serves 4

red curry duck

see variations page 48

Red curry paste is readily available in most grocery stores, and is a fantastic way to add flavor to a dish. If it is too spicy, add a drop more coconut milk to make it a little milder. This recipe uses meat that has already been roasted, but you could also use broiled meat. Serve this dish with rice.

2 tbsp. peanut or vegetable oil
2 cloves garlic, finely chopped
1 oz. fresh ginger, finely chopped
4 scallions, cut into bite-size pieces
2 tbsp. red curry paste
8 oz. fresh shitake mushrooms, sliced

8 oz. stringless green beans, cut into
   bite-size pieces
1/2 large roast duck, flesh finely sliced
2 tbsp. light soy sauce
1/2 cup full-fat coconut milk
1 small bunch fresh cilantro, chopped

Heat a wok until a drop of water evaporates in a second or two. Add the oil, garlic, ginger, and scallions and stir-fry until fragrant and golden. Add the red curry paste and stir-fry for a minute more. Add the shitake mushrooms and green beans and toss for 1 to 2 minutes, until the mushrooms begin to soften.

Add the duck, soy sauce, and coconut milk and bring to a simmer, stirring to combine the ingredients. Stir-fry until the duck is heated through and the beans are tender. Stir through the chopped cilantro and serve.

Serves 4

duck with asian greens & plum sauce

see variations page 49

Plum sauce is a viscous, slightly spicy, sweet, and sour tasting sauce that is often used as a condiment in Chinese cooking. It is readily available in jars at grocery stores, specialty markets, or online, and it pairs well with duck. This recipe is a great way to use up leftover cooked meat and can be served with rice.

2 tbsp. peanut or vegetable oil
1 tsp. five-spice powder
2 cloves garlic, peeled and finely chopped
1 oz. fresh ginger, finely chopped
8 scallions, cut into bite-size pieces

1 bunch Chinese broccoli (see Glossary, page 280), cut into bite-size pieces
1/2 large roast duck, flesh finely sliced
1/8 small Chinese cabbage, cut into bite-size pieces
2/3 cup plum sauce

Heat a wok until a drop of water evaporates in a second or two. Add the oil, five-spice powder, garlic, ginger, and scallions, and stir-fry until fragrant and golden.

Add the Chinese broccoli and stir-fry for another minute. Add the duck and toss for 1 to 2 minutes, until the broccoli is just tender. Add the Chinese cabbage and plum sauce and toss until the Chinese cabbage has just wilted. Serve immediately.

Serves 4

thai-style ground chicken

see variations page 50

Ground meats are great for stir-frying — they take up flavor well, they are easy to gauge for doneness, and they cook very quickly. Holy basil is a variety of basil with a hot, peppery taste; if unavailable, try using regular basil with a couple of pinches of ground black pepper. Serve this dish with steamed greens and rice.

2 tbsp. peanut or vegetable oil
4 cloves garlic, finely chopped
2–3 long red chiles, seeded and finely sliced
2 bird's eye chiles, seeded and finely sliced
4 scallions, finely sliced
1 lb. ground chicken
1 lb. green beans, topped and tailed, and
    finely sliced

2 tbsp. light soy sauce
1 tbsp. dark soy sauce
1 tbsp. oyster sauce
1 tbsp. sweet chili sauce
1 bunch fresh holy basil leaves (see Glossary,
    page 280)

Heat a wok until a drop of water evaporates in a second or two. Add the oil, garlic, chiles, and scallions, and stir-fry until fragrant and beginning to color. Add the ground chicken and stir-fry for 3 to 4 minutes, breaking up any lumps, until almost cooked.

Add the beans, light and dark soy sauces, oyster sauce, and sweet chili sauce and stir-fry for 1 to 2 minutes, until the beans are just tender. Add the holy basil just before serving.

Serves 4

szechuan pepper chicken

see variations page 51

Also known as Chinese coriander, Szechuan peppercorns are commonly used across a range of cuisines, including Tibetan, Nepalese, and Indian, as well as Chinese. They are not related to black peppercorns, and have a lemony, rather than peppery, flavor. They leave a tingly numbness in the mouth, a little like chile. Serve the dish with rice.

1/4 cup light soy sauce
1 tbsp. sesame oil
1 tbsp. chili sauce
2 cloves garlic, finely chopped
1 oz. fresh ginger, finely chopped
1 lb. chicken fillet, cut into bite-size pieces

3 tbsp. peanut or vegetable oil
2 tsp. Szechuan peppercorns
2 long red chiles, seeded and finely sliced
4 scallions, cut into bite-size pieces
2 large heads broccoli, cut into bite-size florets
2–3 tbsp. water, if needed

Combine the soy sauce, sesame oil, chili sauce, garlic, and ginger in a bowl and add the chicken pieces, tossing gently to coat. Let marinate for 10 minutes.

Heat a wok until a drop of water evaporates in a second or two. Add the oil, Szechuan peppercorns, and red chiles, and stir-fry for 10 seconds before adding the scallions, chicken, and marinade. Stir-fry for a few minutes more, then add the broccoli and stir-fry for 3 to 4 minutes, adding a little water if needed, until the broccoli is tender and the chicken is cooked through. Serve immediately.

Serves 4

honey & lemon turkey

see variations page 52

Turkey is a wonderful meat to use in stir-fries. Mildly flavored and low in fat, it provides the basis of a healthy, fresh meal. Because it is very low in fat, it can become dry, so it is essential not to overcook it. Serve this dish with noodles or rice.

2 tbsp. peanut or vegetable oil
1 medium yellow onion, halved lengthwise,
    and sliced
1 oz. fresh ginger, finely chopped
2 medium carrots, sliced
8 oz. button mushrooms, sliced
1 lb. turkey breast, cut into bite-size pieces

6 baby bok choy, cut into bite-size pieces
2 tbsp. honey
zest and juice of 1 lemon
3 tbsp. light soy sauce
1 tsp. cornstarch
1/4 cup cold water
sprigs of fresh cilantro

Heat a wok until a drop of water evaporates in a second or two. Add the oil, onion, and ginger and stir-fry until fragrant and beginning to color. Add the carrots and mushrooms, tossing for 2 to 3 minutes, until the mushrooms have softened. Add the turkey and stir-fry until just cooked.

Add the bok choy, honey, lemon zest and juice, and soy sauce and stir-fry until the bok choy begins to wilt. Mix the cornstarch and water, add it to the wok, and stir immediately to prevent lumps from forming. Continue cooking for about 1 minute, until the sauce is thick and bubbling. Serve immediately, garnished with cilantro.

Serves 4

duck with basil, chile & cashews

see variations page 53

Cooking the duck breasts skin-side down for most of the cooking time will render the fat from the skin, leaving it golden and crisp. Some of the fat can then be retained for cooking the stir-fry.

4 small duck breasts, skin scored
1 tsp. five-spice powder
1/2 tsp. salt
1 long green chile, seeded and finely sliced
1 long red chile, seeded and finely sliced
2 cloves garlic, finely chopped
1 medium yellow onion, halved lengthwise, and chopped
2 carrots, sliced

1 large red bell pepper, cut into bite-size pieces
1 head of broccoli, cut into bite-size florets
3 tbsp. light soy sauce
2 tbsp. hoisin sauce
1 (8-oz.) can water chestnuts, drained
2–3 tbsp. water, if needed
2/3 cup roasted cashews, chopped
1 bunch fresh basil, chopped

Sprinkle the duck breasts with the five-spice powder. Salt them and put them, skin-side down, into a wok over a medium heat. Cook the duck breasts for about 12 minutes, until all the fat renders out of the skin and the skin become crisp, then turn them over and cook for a few minutes longer. Remove them from the wok to a plate and let rest.

Discard all but 2 tablespoons of fat from the wok and heat it to just smoking. Add the chiles, garlic, and onion and stir-fry until fragrant and golden. Add the carrots and bell pepper and toss for 2 to 3 minutes.

Add the broccoli to the wok and toss for 1 to 2 minutes before adding the soy sauce and hoisin sauce. Thinly slice the duck breasts and return them to the wok with any juices and the water chestnuts and toss well, adding a little water, if needed. Toss through half the roasted cashews and basil. Sprinkle with the remaining cashews and serve.

Serves 4

thai basil, onion & chile chicken

see variations page 54

The name Thai basil covers a group of tropical basils that are sweeter in flavor than regular basil. It should be readily available in Asian grocery stores, but if you cannot find it, simply substitute regular Mediterranean basil. Serve this dish with rice.

2 tbsp. peanut or vegetable oil
1 oz. fresh ginger, finely chopped
2 cloves garlic, finely chopped
2–3 long red chiles, seeded and finely sliced
2 medium yellow onions, halved lengthwise, and sliced
1 lb. chicken fillet, sliced

2 medium zucchini, halved lengthwise, and sliced
1/4 cup light soy sauce
2 tbsp. rice wine
1 tbsp. chili sauce
1 tbsp. coconut palm sugar or brown sugar
1 bunch fresh Thai basil leaves

Heat a wok until a drop of water evaporates in a second or two. Add the oil, ginger, garlic, chiles, and onions and stir-fry until fragrant and beginning to color. Add the chicken, tossing for 3 to 4 minutes, until nearly cooked.

Add the zucchini and stir-fry for 2 to 3 minutes, until the zucchini is nearly tender. Add the soy sauce, rice wine, chili sauce, and sugar and stir-fry for 2 to 3 minutes more, until the chicken is cooked and the zucchini is tender. Toss half of the Thai basil through the stir-fry. Garnish with the remaining Thai basil and serve.

Serves 4

turkey with soy & sesame

see variations page 55

Before adding the oil to the pan, quickly toast an additional couple of tablespoons of sesame seeds in the hot wok then set them aside to use as a garnish or condiment for the finished dish. Serve this dish with rice.

1/4 cup light soy sauce
1 tbsp. sesame oil
2 tbsp. sesame seeds
1 tsp. coconut palm sugar or brown sugar
1 lb. turkey breast, cut into bite-size pieces
1 medium yellow onion, halved lengthwise, and sliced

2 tbsp. peanut or vegetable oil
2 cloves garlic, finely chopped
2 medium carrots, sliced
1 red bell pepper, sliced
1 medium zucchini, halved lengthwise, and sliced
2 tbsp. dark soy sauce

Put the light soy sauce, sesame oil, sesame seeds, sugar, and turkey pieces into a bowl and mix well. Let marinate for 10 minutes.

Heat a wok until a drop of water evaporates in a second or two. Add the peanut or vegetable oil, onion, and garlic and stir-fry until fragrant and beginning to color. Add the carrots and bell peppers, tossing for 2 to 3 minutes, until the peppers have started to soften.

Add the turkey and marinade, stir-frying until just cooked before adding the zucchini and dark soy sauce. Stir-fry until the zucchini is tender and the turkey is cooked through. Serve immediately.

Serves 4

lemongrass & ginger turkey

see variations page 56

Lemongrass provides a distinctive lemony flavor to a lot of Asian dishes. It is a tough and fibrous grass plant and the base and tougher outer leaves of the stalk must be removed before finely slicing or chopping the lighter bottom part for cooking. Serve this dish with noodles or rice.

1/4 cup light soy sauce
2 tsp. coconut palm sugar or brown sugar
1 stalk lemongrass, outer leaves and root
    discarded, white part finely chopped
1 1/2 oz. fresh ginger, finely chopped
1 clove garlic, finely chopped
1 lb. turkey breast, cut into bite-size pieces

2 tbsp. peanut or vegetable oil
4 scallions, cut into bite-size pieces
2 green bell peppers, cut into bite-size pieces
2 bunches asparagus, cut into bite-size pieces
1 (8-oz.) can baby corn, drained
1 tsp. cornstarch
1/4 cup cold water

Combine the soy sauce, sugar, lemongrass, ginger, and garlic in a bowl and add the turkey pieces, tossing gently to coat. Let marinate for 10 minutes.

Heat a wok until a drop of water evaporates in a second or two. Add the peanut or vegetable oil, scallions, and bell peppers and stir-fry until just starting to color. Add the turkey and marinade and stir-fry for 3 to 4 minutes, until just cooked. Add the asparagus and toss until crisp-tender before adding the baby corn.

Mix the cornstarch and water, add it to the wok, and stir immediately to prevent lumps from forming. Cook the sauce for about 1 minute, until it is thick and bubbling. Serve immediately.

Serves 4

tamarind duck

see variations page 57

Tamarind adds a delicious sour and slightly sweet taste to this dish. If tamarind paste is unavailable, try soaking a couple of dried dates until soft and process them in a blender with two tablespoons of lime juice for a substitute that's similar in flavor and texture. Serve this dish with rice.

2 tbsp. peanut or vegetable oil
2 cloves garlic, finely chopped
1 oz. fresh ginger, finely chopped
1 large red onion, halved lengthwise, and sliced
1 large green bell pepper, sliced
1 large head broccoli, cut into bite-size florets
1/2 large roast duck, flesh finely sliced

2 tbsp. tamarind paste
2 tbsp. light soy sauce
1 tbsp. coconut palm sugar or brown sugar
1 tbsp. fish sauce
2–3 tbsp. water, if needed
8 oz. tatsoi leaves (see Glossary, page 280)

Heat a wok until a drop of water evaporates in a second or two. Add the peanut or vegetable oil, garlic, ginger, and red onion and stir-fry until fragrant and golden. Add the bell pepper and broccoli and stir-fry for 1 to 2 minutes until the broccoli is just tender.

Add the duck, tamarind paste, soy sauce, sugar, and fish sauce and toss until the duck is heated through, adding water if needed. Add the tatsoi, stir-frying until it has wilted.

Serves 4

malaysian peanut chicken

see variations page 58

Peanut sauce, often served with satay (meat skewers), is very popular in Asian cooking. The sauce will keep in a sealed container in the refrigerator for about a week. For extra texture, try using crunchy peanut butter. Serve this dish with rice or noodles.

1 medium red onion, halved lengthwise, and chopped

4 dried red chiles, seeded and soaked in hot water for 5 minutes

2 cloves garlic

1 oz. galangal, chopped (see Glossary, page 281)

1 stalk lemongrass, outer leaves and root discarded, white part roughly chopped

5 tbsp. peanut or vegetable oil, divided

1 tbsp. tamarind paste

2 tbsp. coconut palm sugar or brown sugar

1/4 cup peanut butter

1 cup water

salt, to taste

1 lb. skinless chicken thigh, cut into bite-size pieces

6 scallions, cut into bite-size pieces

1 large red bell pepper, sliced

8 oz. snow peas, topped and tailed

1 (8-oz.) can pineapple pieces, drained

8 oz. mung bean sprouts

Combine the red onion, soaked chiles, garlic, galangal, and lemongrass in a food processor and process until smooth, then add 3 tablespoons peanut or vegetable oil and process to combine. Place a saucepan over medium heat, add the paste, and cook for 4 to 5 minutes, stirring often, until the paste is fragrant and darker in color. Add the tamarind paste, sugar, peanut butter, and water; mix well; and simmer for 5 minutes, until the sauce has thickened. Remove from the heat, season to taste with salt, and set aside.

Heat a wok until a drop of water evaporates in a second or two. Add 2 tablespoons peanut or vegetable oil and the chicken. Stir-fry for 2 to 3 minutes, until the chicken is partly cooked, then add the scallions and bell pepper and stir-fry for another 3 to 4 minutes, until the chicken is cooked and the pepper is tender.

Add the peanut sauce, snow peas, pineapple pieces, and bean sprouts to the wok and stir-fry for 1 to 2 minutes, until the snow peas are crisp-tender and the chicken is cooked.

Serves 4

chinese-style duck

see variations page 59

Fresh shitake mushrooms can be found in many stores or online. If fresh shitakes
are unavailable, you can substitute dried, reconstituted shitake mushrooms by soaking
1 1/2 ounces of dried shitake mushrooms in enough hot water to cover for 30 minutes.
Serve this dish with rice.

2 tbsp. peanut or vegetable oil
2 cloves garlic, finely chopped
1 oz. fresh ginger, finely chopped
1 large yellow onion, halved lengthwise,
   and sliced
8 oz. fresh shitake mushrooms, sliced
8 oz. button mushrooms, sliced

1/2 large roast duck, flesh finely sliced
2 tbsp. oyster sauce
2 tbsp. light soy sauce
2 tbsp. hoisin sauce
2–3 tbsp. water
8 oz. snow peas, topped and tailed
1 (8-oz.) can water chestnuts, drained

Heat a wok until a drop of water evaporates in a second or two. Add the oil, garlic, ginger,
and onion and stir-fry until fragrant and golden. Add the shitake and button mushrooms and
stir-fry for 1 to 2 minutes, until the mushrooms are starting to color and soften.

Add the duck, oyster sauce, soy sauce, hoisin sauce, and water and toss until the duck is just
heated through. Add the snow peas and water chestnuts, stir-frying until the snow peas are
just tender.

Serves 4

orange & chile duck

see variations page 60

Orange pairs deliciously with duck. For an extra boost of citrus flavor, try substituting a tablespoon of orange marmalade for the sugar in this recipe, or substitute the entire orange with a mandarin instead. Serve this dish with rice or noodles.

zest and juice of 1 orange
2 tbsp. light soy sauce
1 tbsp. kecap manis (see Glossary, page 281)
1 tbsp. coconut palm sugar or brown sugar
1/2 oz. fresh ginger, finely chopped
2 cloves garlic, finely chopped
1 lb. skinless duck breast, sliced

2 tbsp. peanut or vegetable oil
8 scallions, chopped
3 long red chiles, seeded and finely sliced
1 bunch Chinese broccoli, cut into
    3-in. (7.5-cm.) lengths
1 bunch asparagus, woody ends removed
8 oz. green beans, topped and tailed

Combine the orange zest and juice, light soy sauce, kecap manis, sugar, ginger, garlic, and duck in a bowl and mix well. Let marinate for 10 minutes.

Heat a wok until a drop of water evaporates in a second or two. Add the peanut or vegetable oil and the duck, reserving the marinade, and stir-fry until just beginning to color. Add the scallions and chiles, tossing for 3 to 4 minutes, until the duck is nearly cooked.

Add the Chinese broccoli and stir-fry for 1 minute. Add the reserved marinade, asparagus, and green beans and toss for another 1 to 2 minutes, until the duck is cooked and the vegetables are crisp-tender.

Serves 4

turkey & vegetables with teriyaki sauce

see variations page 61

Teriyaki is a Japanese cooking technique where meat is broiled with a glaze of soy sauce, mirin, and sugar. In the West, teriyaki often refers to the flavor, rather than the cooking technique, and teriyaki sauces are commercially available for use in cooking. Serve this dish with rice or noodles.

2 tbsp. peanut or vegetable oil
1 medium yellow onion, halved lengthwise, and sliced
2 stalks celery, sliced
1 clove garlic, finely chopped
1 oz. fresh ginger, finely chopped

2 medium carrots, sliced
1 large red bell pepper, sliced
1 lb. turkey breast, sliced
6 baby bok choy, cut into bite-size pieces
2/3 cup teriyaki sauce
sprigs of fresh cilantro

Heat a wok until a drop of water evaporates in a second or two. Add the oil, onion, celery, garlic, and ginger and stir-fry until fragrant and beginning to color. Add the carrots and bell pepper and toss for 2 to 3 minutes, until the vegetables have just softened. Add the turkey and stir-fry until just cooked.

Add the bok choy and teriyaki sauce and stir-fry until the bok choy begins to wilt and everything is coated with sauce. Garnish with cilantro and serve immediately with rice.

Serves 4

turkey & broccoli with coconut

see variations page 62

Fish sauce is used as a seasoning in many Asian dishes; it is an extremely salty condiment made from fermented fish and gives dishes a mildly fishy taste. It can be found in the Asian food aisle of the grocery store. Substitute salt to taste if fish sauce is unavailable. Serve this dish with plenty of rice to soak up the sauce.

1/2 cup coconut milk
2 tbsp. fish sauce
2 Kaffir lime leaves, shredded (see Glossary, page 281)
1 tbsp. chili sauce
2 tsp. coconut palm sugar or brown sugar
1/2 cup shredded coconut
2 tbsp. peanut or vegetable oil

1/2 small bunch fresh cilantro, leaves picked, stems finely chopped
2 cloves garlic, finely chopped
1 oz. fresh ginger, finely chopped
6 scallions, cut into bite-size pieces
2 medium heads broccoli, cut into bite-size florets
1 lb. turkey breast, sliced
8 oz. snow peas, topped and tailed

Combine the coconut milk, fish sauce, Kaffir lime leaves, chili sauce, and sugar in a bowl and set aside.

Heat a wok until a drop of water evaporates in a second or two. Add the shredded coconut and toss until fragrant and toasted, tip into a bowl, and set aside. Return the wok to the heat.

Add the oil, finely chopped cilantro stems, garlic, ginger, and scallions and stir-fry until fragrant and golden. Add the broccoli and stir-fry for 2 to 3 minutes, until it starts to color.

Add the turkey and toss until nearly cooked. Add the snow peas and coconut milk mixture and bring to a boil, simmering until the turkey is cooked and the vegetables are crisp-tender. Garnish with the toasted coconut and fresh cilantro leaves. Serve immediately.

Serves 4

turkey with red chile & kaffir lime

see variations page 63

The leaves from the Kaffir lime tree have a distinctive hourglass shape, with two leaves joined head to tail, and a strong lime flavor. They can be purchased fresh, frozen, dried, or in jars. Fresh and frozen leaves have the best flavor, while those stored in jars have a stronger flavor. Serve this dish with rice.

1/4 cup light soy sauce
1 tbsp. lime juice
2 tsp. coconut palm sugar or brown sugar
4 Kaffir lime leaves, finely shredded
2 bird's eye chiles, seeded and finely chopped
1 clove garlic, finely chopped
1 lb. turkey breast, sliced

2 tbsp. peanut or vegetable oil
4 scallions, cut into bite-size pieces
2 long red chiles, seeded and finely sliced
8 oz. Chinese cabbage, shredded
8 oz. baby spinach
2–3 tbsp. water, if needed

Combine the soy sauce, lime juice, sugar, lime leaves, bird's eye chiles, and garlic in a bowl and add the turkey pieces, tossing gently to coat. Let marinate for 10 minutes.

Heat a wok until a drop of water evaporates in a second or two. Add the peanut or vegetable oil, scallions, and red chiles and stir-fry until just starting to color. Add the turkey and marinade and stir-fry for 3 to 4 minutes, until just cooked.

Add the Chinese cabbage, baby spinach and a little water, if needed, stir-frying until just wilted. Serve immediately.

Serves 4

chicken & snow peas in oyster sauce

see variations page 64

Oyster sauce is a thick brown sauce made from stewed, reduced oysters with sugar and salt. It has a distinctive savory flavor, and is readily available in the Asian food aisle of most grocery stores. Serve this dish with rice.

2 tbsp. peanut or vegetable oil
1 oz. fresh ginger, finely chopped
2 cloves garlic, finely chopped
8 scallions, chopped

1 lb. chicken fillet, sliced
1 lb. snow peas, topped and tailed
1 (8-oz.) can water chestnuts, drained
1/2 cup oyster sauce

Heat a wok until a drop of water evaporates in a second or two. Add the oil, ginger, garlic, and scallions and stir-fry until fragrant and beginning to color. Add the chicken, tossing for 2 to 3 minutes, until the chicken is nearly cooked.

Add the snow peas, stir-fry for 1 to 2 minutes, then add the water chestnuts and oyster sauce and cook for a minute more, until the chicken is cooked and the snow peas are tender.

Serves 4

chicken & shitake mushrooms with galangal

see variations page 65

Galangal is a close relative of ginger, and it has a similar look and flavor. It can be found fresh in Asian grocery stores or online, or occasionally, ready minced in jars. If unavailable, substitute with fresh ginger in equal amounts. Serve this dish with rice.

2 tbsp. peanut or vegetable oil
1 1/2 oz. fresh galangal, finely chopped
2 cloves garlic, finely chopped
1 medium yellow onion, halved lengthwise,
    and sliced
1 lb. fresh shitake mushrooms, sliced
1 lb. chicken fillet, sliced

6 baby bok choy, chopped
2 tbsp. light soy sauce
2 tbsp. dark soy
1 tsp. chili sauce
2 tsp. coconut palm sugar or brown sugar
1 bunch fresh holy basil leaves

Heat a wok until a drop of water evaporates in a second or two. Add the peanut or vegetable oil, galangal, garlic, and onion and stir-fry until fragrant and beginning to color. Add the shitake mushrooms, tossing for 2 to 3 minutes, until they begin to color and soften.

Add the chicken and stir-fry for 2 to 3 minutes, until it is nearly cooked. Add the bok choy, soy sauces, chili sauce, and sugar and stir-fry for 2 to 3 minutes more, until the chicken is cooked and the bok choy is tender. Toss half of the holy basil leaves through the stir-fry. Garnish with the remaining holy basil leaves.

Serves 4

variations

chili paste & chicken (pad phet)

see base recipe page 15

green curry paste & chicken
Prepare the basic recipe, but substitute 3 green chiles, chopped, for the red chiles, and
1 tablespoon of green curry paste for the chili paste.

chili paste & turkey
Substitute 1 pound of turkey breast, cut into bite-size pieces, for the chicken. Complete the
recipe as directed.

chili paste, chicken & noodles
Prepare 12 ounces of egg noodles according to package directions and add to the wok with
the bok choy and bean sprouts, then complete the recipe as directed. There is no need to
serve this variation with rice.

chili paste, chicken & eggplant
Prepare the basic recipe, but substitute one large eggplant, halved lengthwise and thinly
sliced, for the cauliflower.

hoisin duck with spinach

see base recipe page 16

hoisin chicken with spinach
Substitute the finely sliced flesh of 1/2 large roast chicken for the duck. Complete the recipe as directed.

hoisin duck with spinach & chile
Prepare the basic recipe, and add 2 long red chiles, seeded and finely sliced, to the wok with the garlic, ginger, and scallions.

hoisin duck with bok choy
Prepare the basic recipe, but substitute 6 chopped baby bok choy for the spinach. Complete the recipe as directed.

hoisin duck with spinach & ginger
Increase the fresh ginger to 1 1/2 ounces, and add 1 teaspoon sugar to the wok with the sauces.

variations

red curry duck

see base recipe page 18

green curry duck
Prepare the basic recipe, but substitute 2 tablespoons green curry paste for the red curry paste.

yellow curry duck
Prepare the basic recipe, but substitute 2 tablespoons yellow curry paste for the red curry paste.

red curry turkey
Substitute 1 pound cooked, sliced turkey for the duck. Complete the recipe as directed.

red curry duck with noodles
Prepare 12 ounces of fresh egg noodles according to package directions and add to the wok with the duck, soy sauce, and coconut milk. Complete the recipe as directed. There is no need to serve this variation with rice.

variations

duck with asian greens & plum sauce

see base recipe page 20

duck with bell peppers & plum sauce
Prepare the basic recipe, but substitute 1 red and 1 yellow bell pepper, both cut into bite-size pieces, for the Chinese broccoli.

duck with chili, broccoli & plum sauce
Add 2 seeded and finely sliced red chiles to the wok with the garlic, ginger, and scallions, and substitute 1 large head broccoli, cut into bite-size florets, for the Chinese broccoli. Complete the recipe as directed.

chicken with asian greens & plum sauce
Prepare the basic recipe, but substitute the finely sliced flesh of 1/2 roast chicken for the duck.

duck with asian greens, plum sauce & sesame
Add 2 tablespoons sesame seeds to the wok with the ginger, garlic, and scallions, and 1 tablespoon sesame oil with the soy and plum sauces. Complete the recipe as directed.

variations

thai-style ground chicken

see base recipe page 21

mongolian-style ground chicken
Prepare the basic recipe, but substitute 1 ounce finely chopped fresh ginger for the bird's eye chiles; 1 pound Chinese cabbage, shredded, for the green beans; and 2 tablespoons hoisin sauce for the sweet chili sauce.

thai-style ground chicken & noodles
Prepare 8 ounces of dry rice noodles according to package directions and add to the wok with the green beans, allowing them to heat through before serving. There is no need to serve this variation with rice.

thai-style ground turkey
Substitute 1 pound ground turkey for the ground chicken. Complete the recipe as directed.

spicy thai-style ground chicken
Increase the bird's eye chiles to 3 or 4, depending on taste, and substitute 1 to 2 tablespoons of chili sauce, to taste, for the sweet chili sauce.

szechuan pepper chicken

see base recipe page 22

szechuan pepper duck
Prepare the basic recipe, but substitute 1 pound skinless duck, cut into bite-size pieces, for the chicken fillet.

szechuan pepper turkey
Prepare the basic recipe, but substitute 1 pound turkey breast, cut into bite-size pieces, for the chicken fillet.

black pepper chicken
Prepare the basic recipe, but substitute 2 teaspoons crushed black peppercorns for the Szechuan peppercorns.

hot chili chicken
Prepare the basic recipe, but substitute 2 teaspoons dried chili flakes for the Szechuan peppercorns.

honey & lemon turkey

see base recipe page 24

spicy honey & lemon turkey
Add 2 teaspoons chili paste (or more to taste) to the wok with the onion and ginger, and complete the recipe as directed .

honey & lemon chicken
Prepare the basic recipe, but substitute 1 pound chicken fillet, cut into bite-size pieces for the turkey.

sweet chili & lemon turkey
Prepare the basic recipe, but substitute 1/4 cup sweet chili sauce for the honey.

honey, ginger & lime turkey
Increase the fresh ginger to 1 1/2 ounces and substitute the zest and juice of 1 fresh lime for the lemon zest and juice. Complete the recipe as directed.

duck with basil, chile & cashews

see base recipe page 26

duck with cilantro, chile & peanuts
Prepare the basic recipe, but substitute 2/3 cup roasted peanuts for the cashews and a bunch of fresh cilantro, chopped, for the basil.

chicken with basil, chile & cashews
Prepare the basic recipe, but substitute 4 small chicken breasts for the duck breasts. Add 2 tablespoons peanut or vegetable oil to the wok before cooking the chicken breasts, because they do not contain as much fat as the duck breasts.

duck with basil, chile & lime
Add the zest and juice of 1 fresh lime and 1 tablespoon of sugar to the wok with the soy and hoisin sauces. Complete the recipe as directed.

turkey with basil, lime & fried shallots
Omit the duck breasts and cashews. Stir-fry 1 pound thinly sliced turkey breast in 2 tablespoons peanut or vegetable oil until just cooked, and set aside on a plate to rest. Complete the recipe as directed, adding the zest and juice of 1 fresh lime and 1 tablespoon of sugar to the wok with the soy and hoisin sauces, and substituting 2/3 cup fried shallots for the cashews.

variations

thai basil, onion & chile chicken

see base recipe page 28

thai basil, onion & chile chicken noodles
Prepare 8 ounces of dry rice noodles according to package directions and add to the wok with the soy sauce, allowing them to heat through before serving. There is no need to serve this variation with rice.

thai basil, onion & ginger chicken
Omit the fresh chiles, chili sauce, and sugar. Increase the ginger to 1 1/2 ounces and add 2 tablespoons kecap manis to the wok with the soy sauce.

thai basil, garlic & chile chicken
Prepare the basic recipe, but halve the onion and increase the garlic to 4 cloves, peeled and finely chopped.

cilantro, onion & chile chicken with lime
Add 2 finely shredded Kaffir lime leaves to the wok with the chicken, and substitute 1 bunch chopped fresh cilantro for the Thai basil. Serve with lime wedges.

turkey with soy & sesame

see base recipe page 29

turkey with soy & garlic
Prepare the basic recipe, but omit the sesame seeds and oil and increase the garlic to
4 cloves, finely chopped.

turkey with sweet soy & ginger
Prepare the basic recipe, but omit the sesame seeds and oil and the dark soy sauce. Reduce
the light soy sauce to 2 tablespoons and add 1 1/2 ounces finely chopped fresh ginger to
the wok with the onion and garlic. Replace the dark soy sauce with 1/4 cup kecap manis.

chicken with soy & sesame
Prepare the basic recipe, but substitute 1 pound sliced chicken fillet for the turkey.

chicken with soy, chile & sesame
Prepare the basic recipe, but substitute 1 pound sliced chicken fillet for the turkey, and
add 2 seeded and finely sliced red chiles to the wok with the garlic and onion.

turkey & noodle with soy & sesame
Prepare 12 ounces of egg noodles according to package directions and add to the wok
with the zucchini. Complete the recipe as directed. There is no need to serve this
variation with rice.

variations

lemongrass & ginger turkey

see base recipe page 30

lemongrass & galangal turkey
Prepare the basic recipe, but substitute 1 1/2 ounces galangal, finely chopped, for the ginger.

lemongrass, ginger & chile turkey
Prepare the basic recipe, but add 2 seeded and finely sliced red chiles to the wok with the scallions and green bell peppers.

lemongrass & ginger duck
Prepare the basic recipe, but substitute 1 pound skinless duck breast, cut into bite-size pieces, for the turkey.

lemongrass, ginger & cilantro turkey
Prepare the basic recipe, and add 1 bunch chopped fresh cilantro to the stir-fry just before serving.

tamarind duck

see base recipe page 32

tamarind duck & coconut
Prepare the basic recipe, and add 1/2 cup coconut milk to the wok with the tamarind paste, soy sauce, and fish sauce.

tamarind duck & bok choy
Prepare the basic recipe, but substitute 4 chopped baby bok choy for the tatsoi.

tamarind duck & ginger
Prepare the basic recipe, but increase the ginger to 1 1/2 ounces, finely chopped, and add 2 teaspoons sugar to the wok with the tamarind paste.

tamarind chicken
Prepare the basic recipe, but substitute the finely sliced flesh of 1/2 large roast chicken for the duck.

malaysian peanut chicken

see base recipe page 34

indonesian peanut chicken
Prepare the basic recipe, but add 2 Kaffir lime leaves; a pinch each of ground nutmeg, cinnamon, cardamom, and cloves; and 2 tablespoons dark soy sauce to the wok with the peanut butter. Replace the water with coconut milk.

thai peanut chicken
Prepare the basic recipe, but add the juice and zest of 1 lime and 2 tablespoons light soy sauce to the wok with the peanut butter. Replace the water with coconut milk.

spicy peanut chicken
Prepare the basic recipe, but add 2 to 3 teaspoons, to taste, of chili paste to the wok with the peanut butter.

malaysian peanut turkey
Prepare the basic recipe, but substitute 1 pound turkey steak, cut into bite-size pieces, for the chicken.

chinese-style duck

see base recipe page 36

chinese-style chicken
Prepare the basic recipe, but substitute the sliced flesh of 1/2 a large roast chicken for the duck.

chinese-style turkey
Prepare the basic recipe, but substitute 1 pound of thinly sliced barbecue turkey for the duck.

chinese-style duck with noodles
Prepare 12 ounces of fresh thin egg noodles according to package directions and add to the wok with the duck. Complete the recipe as directed. There is no need to serve this variation with rice.

spicy chinese-style duck
Prepare the basic recipe, but add 2 seeded and finely sliced red chiles to the wok with the garlic, ginger, and onion and add 1 to 2 tablespoons of chili sauce, to taste, with the duck.

variations

orange & chile duck

see base recipe page 37

lime & chile duck
Prepare the basic recipe, but substitute the zest and juice of 1 fresh lime and 2 finely shredded Kaffir lime leaves for the orange zest and juice in the marinade.

orange & chile chicken
Prepare the basic recipe, but substitute 1 pound sliced, skinless chicken fillet for the duck.

orange & ginger duck
Prepare the basic recipe, but omit the chiles and increase the fresh ginger to 1 1/2 ounces, peeled and finely chopped.

orange & chile duck with thai basil
Prepare the basic recipe, but add 1 bunch of chopped fresh Thai basil to the stir-fry just before serving.

turkey & vegetables with teriyaki sauce

see base recipe page 38

turkey & vegetables with sweet chili sauce
Prepare the basic recipe, but omit the teriyaki sauce. Add 1/2 cup sweet chili sauce,
1 tablespoon light soy sauce, and 2 teaspoons rice wine to the wok with the bok choy
and complete the recipe as directed.

turkey & vegetables with chili sauce
Prepare the basic recipe, but omit the teriyaki sauce and substitute 1/2 cup sweet chili sauce
and 2 to 3 tablespoons chili sauce, to taste.

turkey & vegetables with oyster sauce
Prepare the basic recipe, but substitute 2/3 cup oyster sauce for the teriyaki sauce and stir-fry
until the vegetables are just tender before serving.

chicken & vegetables with teriyaki sauce
Prepare the basic recipe, but substitute 1 pound sliced, skinless chicken fillet for the turkey.

variations

turkey & broccoli with coconut

see base recipe page 40

turkey & bok choy with coconut
Prepare the basic recipe, but omit the broccoli. Add the turkey to the wok after the garlic, ginger, and scallions, and add 8 chopped baby bok choy to the wok with the snow peas.

chicken & broccoli with coconut
Prepare the basic recipe, but substitute 1 pound sliced, skinless chicken fillet for the turkey.

turkey & broccoli with coconut & chili
Prepare the basic recipe, but add 2 to 3 seeded and finely sliced red chiles to the wok with the broccoli.

turkey & mushroom with coconut
Prepare the basic recipe, but substitute 1 pound sliced button mushrooms for the broccoli.

turkey & bell pepper with coconut
Prepare the basic recipe, but substitute 1 red, 1 green, and 1 yellow bell pepper, all sliced, for the broccoli.

turkey with red chile & kaffir lime

see base recipe page 42

chicken with red chile & kaffir lime
Prepare the basic recipe, but substitute 1 pound of sliced, skinless chicken fillet for the turkey.

turkey with ginger & kaffir lime
Prepare the basic recipe, but omit the bird's eye and red chiles and add 1 1/2 ounces fresh ginger, finely chopped, to the marinade with the garlic.

turkey with red chile & kaffir lime, fried shallots & lime
Garnish the stir-fry with 1/2 cup fried shallots and 2 limes, cut into wedges.

turkey with green chile & kaffir lime
Prepare the basic recipe, but omit the bird's eye and red chiles. Add 1 finely chopped green chile to the marinade with the garlic, and 2 seeded and finely sliced green chiles to the wok with the scallions.

chicken & snow peas in oyster sauce

see base recipe page 43

chicken & snow peas in hoisin sauce
Prepare the basic recipe, but substitute 1/2 cup hoisin sauce for the oyster sauce.

duck & snow peas in oyster sauce
Prepare the basic recipe, but substitute 1 pound of sliced, skinless duck breast for the chicken.

chicken & bell peppers in oyster sauce
Prepare the basic recipe, but substitute 3 red bell peppers, thinly sliced, for the snow peas.

chicken, snow peas & noodles in oyster sauce
Prepare 12 ounces of fresh udon noodles according to package directions and add to the wok with the snow peas. Complete the recipe as directed. There is no need to serve this variation with rice.

chicken & shitake mushrooms with galangal

see base recipe page 44

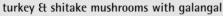

turkey & shitake mushrooms with galangal
Prepare the basic recipe, but substitute 1 pound sliced turkey breast for the chicken.

chicken & zucchini with galangal
Prepare the basic recipe, but omit the shitake mushrooms. Add the chicken to the wok after the galangal, garlic, and onions, and stir-fry until nearly cooked. Add 2 medium zucchini, halved lengthwise and sliced, to the wok with the bok choy.

chicken & shitake mushrooms with galangal & chile
Prepare the basic recipe, but add 2 seeded and finely sliced red chiles to the wok with the shitake mushrooms.

chicken & snow peas with galangal
Prepare the basic recipe, but omit the shitake mushrooms. Add the chicken to the wok after the galangal, garlic, and onions, and stir-fry until nearly cooked before adding 1 pound snow peas, topped and tailed, to the wok with the bok choy.

pork, beef & lamb

Once the realm of the wealthy, these meats are now a popular addition to many Asian meals, stir-fry dishes being no exception. Stir-frying is a wonderful way to showcase your favorite cuts, offering a range of preparation techniques and delicious flavors. To cut extremely thin slices, try freezing the meat for 30 minutes before slicing, because this makes it firmer and easier to slice.

ginger beef with shitake mushrooms

see variations page 101

Dried shitake mushrooms can be found in Asian grocers and or the Asian food aisle of most grocery stores. They soften easily in hot water, and the water they were soaked in can also be added to dishes, because it is full of flavor. Serve this dish with rice.

3 oz. dried, sliced shitake mushrooms
2 tbsp. light soy sauce
1/4 cup oyster sauce
1 tbsp. fish sauce
1 tsp. coconut palm sugar or brown sugar
2 tbsp. peanut or vegetable oil
1 lb. beef sirloin, thinly sliced

1 1/2 oz. fresh ginger, cut into matchsticks
2 cloves garlic, finely chopped
1 medium yellow onion, halved
    lengthwise, and sliced
1 large red bell pepper, cut into
    bite-size pieces
4 scallions, chopped

Put the mushrooms into a bowl and cover with hot water. Allow to sit for 10 minutes before draining, reserving 1/4 cup of the liquid. Combine the light soy sauce, oyster sauce, fish sauce, and sugar in a bowl and stir to dissolve the sugar; set aside.

Heat a wok until a drop of water evaporates in a second or two. Add the oil and the beef and stir-fry for 1 minute until just browned. Add the ginger, garlic, and onion and stir-fry until fragrant and golden. Add the mushrooms and bell pepper and toss until the pepper starts to soften and color. Add the prepared sauce and reserved mushroom liquid. Cook for 1 to 2 minutes, until the beef is cooked through and the sauce slightly reduced, then toss through half the scallions. Sprinkle with the remaining scallions and serve immediately.

Serves 4

ground pork with lemongrass

see variations page 102

Lemongrass can be purchased as fresh stalks or ready minced in jars for convenience. Once opened, jars should be stored in the refrigerator and used within the recommended time. Stalks of fresh lemongrass can be kept with their root ends in water in the refrigerator. Serve this dish with noodles or rice.

2 tbsp. peanut or vegetable oil
1 lb. ground pork
1 stalk lemongrass, outer leaves and root
    discarded, white part finely chopped
1 oz. fresh ginger, finely chopped
1 clove garlic, finely chopped
4 scallions, cut into bite-size pieces

2 carrots, sliced
2 red bell peppers, cut into bite-size pieces
2 bunches broccolini, cut into bite-size pieces
1/4 cup light soy sauce
1 tbsp. fish sauce
2 tsp. coconut palm sugar or brown sugar

Heat a wok until a drop of water evaporates in a second or two. Add the oil and the pork and stir-fry until the pork is browned, breaking up any lumps. Add the lemongrass, ginger, and garlic and stir until fragrant before adding the scallions, carrots, and bell peppers. Stir-fry for 2 to 3 minutes, until just starting to soften.

Add the broccolini, soy sauce, fish sauce, and sugar and stir-fry for 2 to 3 minutes, until the vegetables are crisp-tender. Serve immediately.

Serves 4

lamb with thai basil

see variations page 103

Lamb fillet, loin, or tenderloin can be used in this recipe, because they are very lean and tender, perfect for quick cooking, and full of flavor. Fish sauce is made from fermented fish and has a salty, pungent flavor. Serve this dish with rice.

2 tbsp. peanut or vegetable oil
1 oz. fresh ginger, cut into matchsticks
2 cloves garlic, finely chopped
1 stalk lemongrass, outer leaves and root
    discarded, white part finely chopped
4 scallions, chopped
1 lb. lamb fillet, thinly sliced
1 large carrot, sliced

2 medium zucchini, halved lengthwise
    and sliced
3 tbsp. light soy sauce
1 tbsp. fish sauce
1 tbsp. coconut palm sugar or brown sugar
zest and juice of 1 lime
1 bunch fresh Thai basil leaves

Heat a wok until a drop of water evaporates in a second or two. Add the oil, ginger, garlic, lemongrass, and scallions and stir-fry until fragrant and golden. Add the lamb and toss until it starts to color and cook.

Add the carrot and cook for 1 to 2 minutes more, before adding the zucchini, soy sauce, fish sauce, sugar, and lime zest and juice. Continue stir-frying until the lamb is cooked through and the vegetables are crisp-tender, then toss with half the Thai basil. Sprinkle with the remaining Thai basil and serve immediately.

Serves 4

red curry lamb & eggplant

see variations page 104

Eggplant can take a lot of oil when cooking. If it starts to become too dry, or the curry paste begins to burn, you may find that reducing the heat and adding a little coconut milk can help. Serve this dish with rice.

3 tbsp. peanut or vegetable oil, divided
1 lb. lamb fillet, sliced
1 long red chile, seeded and finely sliced
2 cloves garlic, finely chopped
8 scallions, cut into bite-size pieces
2 tbsp. red curry paste

1 large eggplant, halved and sliced into strips
1/2 cup coconut milk
2 tbsp. fish sauce
1 small bunch fresh cilantro, chopped
1 red chile, finely sliced, to serve

Heat a wok until a drop of water evaporates in a second or two. Add half of the oil and the lamb and stir-fry for 2 to 3 minutes until just cooked. Remove the lamb to a plate, cover, and keep warm.

Add the remaining oil to the wok, heat until smoking, then add the chile, garlic, and scallions and stir until fragrant and golden. Add the red curry paste and fry for 15 seconds more. Add the eggplant and toss for 2 to 3 minutes until it is golden and coated in the red curry paste.

Add the coconut milk and fish sauce to the wok and bring to a simmer, stirring, until the eggplant has softened. Return the lamb and any juices to the wok and stir-fry until the lamb is heated through. Toss through half the cilantro. Sprinkle with the remaining cilantro and the finely sliced red chili.

Serves 4

sticky pork with chinese broccoli

see variations page 105

Take care when stir-frying the pork in this recipe, because the higher sugar content in the marinade may cause it to burn easily. If it begins to burn, reduce the heat a little and continue stir-frying. Kecap Manis is a dark, sticky soy sauce. Serve with rice.

1 lb. pork fillet, sliced
1/4 cup hoisin sauce
2 tbsp. light soy sauce
2 tbsp. kecap manis (see Glossary, page 281)
1 tbsp. rice wine
1 tbsp. coconut palm sugar or brown sugar

2 cloves garlic, finely chopped
2 tbsp. peanut or vegetable oil
8 scallions, cut into bite-size pieces
1 large bunch Chinese broccoli, cut into
    bite-size pieces
1/4 cup water, if needed

Combine the pork, hoisin sauce, soy sauce, kecap manis, rice wine, sugar, and garlic in a bowl and mix well. Set aside for 15 minutes.

Heat a wok until a drop of water evaporates in a second or two. Add the oil and scallions and stir-fry until fragrant and golden. Add the pork and marinade to the wok and toss until the pork starts to color and cook.

Add the Chinese broccoli and stir-fry for 2 to 3 minutes, until the Chinese broccoli begins to wilt and the pork is cooked, adding a little water if necessary. Serve immediately.

Serves 4

crispy beef

see variations page 106

Deep frying can easily be performed in your wok, but draining away hot oil can be extremely dangerous and cause serious burns. Therefore, I recommend using a saucepan for the deep frying in this recipe. Always take extra care around hot oil. Serve this dish with rice.

2 tsp. five-spice powder
2 tbsp. cornstarch
1 lb. beef sirloin, finely sliced
peanut or vegetable oil for deep frying
2 tbsp. peanut or vegetable oil
2 cloves garlic, finely chopped
1/2 oz. fresh ginger, finely chopped
2 long red chiles, seeded and finely sliced

4 scallions, cut into bite-size pieces
2 large red bell peppers, sliced
2 tbsp. sweet chili sauce
2 tbsp. ketchup
1 tbsp. rice wine
1/4 cup light soy sauce
4 baby bok choy, chopped

Combine the five-spice powder and the cornstarch in a bowl. Pat the beef slices dry with paper towels, put in the bowl, and toss to coat. Heat 2 inches (5 cm.) of peanut or vegetable oil in a large saucepan until the end of a wooden chopstick bubbles when dipped in. Fry the beef in 3 batches, for 2 to 3 minutes each batch, until the beef is golden and crisp. Remove each batch from the wok using a slotted spoon and put on paper towels to drain. Remove the oil from the heat and let cool before discarding.

Heat a wok until a drop of water evaporates in a second or two. Add 2 tablespoons oil, garlic, ginger, chiles, and scallions and stir-fry until fragrant and beginning to color.

Add the bell pepper to the wok and toss for 1 to 2 minutes until it begins to soften. Add the chili sauce, ketchup, rice wine, and soy sauce to the wok and bring the sauce to a simmer, stirring to combine. Add the beef and bok choy to the wok, toss to coat everything in sauce, and cook until the bok choy has wilted and the beef is hot. Serve immediately.

Serves 4

beef with red chili paste

see variations page 107

There are many varieties of red chili paste on the market. Some of them are sweeter, others are hotter; it's worth trying a few different types to find the one that suits both your taste buds and heat tolerance. Serve this dish with rice.

1 lb. beef sirloin, sliced
2 tbsp. Thai-style chili paste
2 tbsp. peanut or vegetable oil
1 large red onion, halved lengthwise, and sliced
2 stalks celery, sliced

1 large head of broccoli, cut into
    bite-size florets
1/4 cup water
2 tbsp. light soy sauce
1 tbsp. fish sauce
4 baby bok choy, chopped

Combine the beef and chili paste in a bowl and set aside for 10 minutes to marinate. Heat a wok until a drop of water evaporates in a second or two. Add the oil and red onion and stir-fry for 1 to 2 minutes, until the onion is just starting to color. Add the beef and toss for another 1 to 2 minutes, until the chili paste is fragrant and the beef partly cooked.

Add the celery, broccoli, and water to the wok and stir-fry for 1 to 2 minutes, then add the light soy sauce, fish sauce, and bok choy. Continue to stir-fry until the bok choy begins to wilt and the beef is cooked.

Serves 4

sweet & sour pork

see variations page 108

Sweet and sour is a classic stir-fry dish that has always been popular. Preparing the sauce in advance means this meal will be quick and easy to get to the table. Serve with plenty of rice to soak up the sauce.

1/4 cup white vinegar
1/4 cup white sugar
2 tbsp. sweet chili sauce
2 tbsp. light soy sauce
1 (15-oz.) can pineapple pieces, drained,
    1/4 cup juice reserved
2 tbsp. cornstarch

2 tbsp. peanut or vegetable oil
8 scallions, cut into bite-size pieces
2 cloves garlic, finely chopped
1 lb. pork fillet, sliced
2 green bell peppers, cut into bite-size pieces
1 large carrot, sliced
8 oz. snow peas, topped and tailed

Combine the white vinegar, sugar, sweet chili sauce, and light soy sauce in a saucepan over medium heat. Bring to a boil and stir until the sugar dissolves. Reduce the heat to a simmer, whisk together the reserved pineapple juice and cornstarch, and add to the saucepan, whisking until the sauce has thickened. Remove from the heat and set aside.

Heat a wok until a drop of water evaporates in a second or two. Add the oil, scallions, and garlic and stir-fry until fragrant and golden. Add the pork and toss until it begins to color and cook. Add the bell pepper and carrot and stir-fry for 2 to 3 minutes, until the vegetables start to soften. Add the sauce, pineapple pieces, and snow peas and simmer until the pork is cooked through and the vegetables are crisp-tender.

Serves 4

lamb & squash with green chile & lime

see variations page 109

The Kaffir lime leaves in this recipe can be substituted for extra lime zest if the leaves are unavailable. Try serving this dish with extra wedges of lime and some fried shallots, as well as some steamed rice.

2 tbsp. peanut or vegetable oil
2 cloves garlic, finely chopped
1 oz. fresh ginger, finely chopped
2 long green chiles, seeded and finely sliced
2 Kaffir lime leaves, shredded
1 large red onion, halved lengthwise, and sliced
1 lb. lamb fillet, sliced
1 lb. yellow squash, sliced

1 medium zucchini, halved lengthwise
   and sliced
3 tbsp. light soy sauce
3 tbsp. kecap manis
2 tsp. coconut palm sugar or brown sugar
zest and juice of 1 lime
1 small bunch fresh cilantro, chopped
1 green chile, sliced, optional

Heat a wok until a drop of water evaporates in a second or two. Add the oil, garlic, ginger, chiles, lime leaves, and red onion and stir-fry until fragrant and golden. Add the lamb and toss until it starts to color and cook.

Add the yellow squash and zucchini and cook for 1 to 2 minutes before adding the light soy sauce, kecap manis, sugar, and lime zest and juice. Stir-fry until the beef is cooked and the vegetables are crisp-tender. Toss through half the cilantro. Sprinkle with the remaining cilantro and an extra green chile, if desired.

Serves 4

beef with bamboo shoots & baby corn

see variations page 110

Baby corn is usually available fresh in grocery stores; if it is unavailable fresh it can also be purchased in cans, and as with bamboo shoots, it just needs to be drained and it is ready to use. Serve this dish with rice.

2 tbsp. peanut or vegetable oil
2 cloves garlic, finely chopped
1 stalk lemongrass, outer leaves and root
    discarded, white part finely chopped
4 scallions, chopped
1 lb. beef fillet, sliced

2 (8-oz.) cans bamboo shoots, drained
8 oz. fresh baby corn, sliced
1/4 cup light soy sauce
2 tbsp. kecap manis
1 bunch fresh cilantro, chopped

Heat a wok until a drop of water evaporates in a second or two. Add the oil, garlic, lemongrass, and scallions and stir-fry until fragrant and golden. Add the beef and toss until it starts to color and cook.

Add the bamboo shoots and baby corn and cook for 1 to 2 minutes, then add the soy sauce and kecap manis. Continue stir-frying until the beef is cooked through and the vegetables are crisp-tender, then toss through half the cilantro. Sprinkle with the remaining cilantro and serve immediately.

Serves 4

ground lamb & water chestnuts in hoisin sauce

see variations page 111

Water chestnuts provide a crisp, juicy texture to the dishes they're added to. They are available in cans from Asian food stores and some grocery stores; they just need to be drained and they're ready to use. Serve the lamb in lettuce cups with rice or noodles.

2 tbsp. peanut or vegetable oil
1 lb. ground lamb
1 stalk lemongrass, outer leaves and root discarded, white part finely chopped
1 oz. fresh ginger, finely chopped
2 cloves garlic, finely chopped
4 scallions, cut into bite-size pieces

2 (8-oz.) cans water chestnuts, drained and chopped
1/2 cup hoisin sauce
1 tbsp. fish sauce
2 tsp. coconut palm sugar or brown sugar
1 iceberg lettuce, separated into individual leaves to make cups
1/2 cup roasted peanuts, chopped

Heat a wok until a drop of water evaporates in a second or two. Add the oil and the lamb and stir-fry until browned, breaking up any lumps. Add the lemongrass, ginger, and garlic and stir-fry until fragrant. Add the scallions and stir for 1 minute more until just starting to soften.

Add the water chestnuts, hoisin sauce, fish sauce, and sugar and stir-fry for 1 to 2 minutes, until everything is combined and heated through. Serve immediately in lettuce cups, sprinkled with chopped peanuts.

Serves 4

chile & basil beef with peanuts

see variations page 112

This recipe calls for beef fillet, which is the leanest and most tender cut of beef. If it is unavailable, it can be easily substituted with any lean, tender cut of beef such as sirloin or rump. Serve this dish with rice or noodles.

2 tbsp. peanut or vegetable oil
2 cloves garlic, finely chopped
1 oz. fresh ginger, finely chopped
2 bird's eye chiles, seeded and finely sliced
1 large red onion, halved lengthwise, and sliced
1 lb. beef fillet, sliced
1 large head broccoli, cut into bite-size florets

2 (8-oz.) cans water chestnuts, drained
1/4 cup oyster sauce
2 tbsp. light soy sauce
2–3 tbsp. water, if needed
1 bunch fresh basil, chopped
2/3 cup roasted peanuts, chopped
fresh basil leaves, if desired

Heat a wok until a drop of water evaporates in a second or two. Add the oil, garlic, ginger, chiles, and onion and stir-fry until fragrant and golden. Add the beef and toss until it starts to color and cook.

Add the broccoli and cook for 1 to 2 minutes more, then add the water chestnuts, oyster sauce, and soy sauce. Continue stir-frying until the beef is cooked through and the vegetables are crisp-tender, adding a little water if necessary. Toss through half the basil and the peanuts. Sprinkle with the remaining basil and peanuts, and serve immediately. Garnish with whole basil leaves, if desired.

Serves 4

pork belly & shrimp with ginger & garlic

see variations page 113

The fat in the pork belly should mean that it fries golden and crisp. If you struggle to get your wok hot enough, fry the pork in small batches instead of one large batch to prevent the wok cooling and the meat stewing. Serve this dish with noodles or rice.

10 oz. pork belly, very finely sliced
2 tbsp. peanut or vegetable oil, divided
1 1/2 oz. fresh ginger, cut into matchsticks
3 cloves garlic, finely chopped
1 medium red onion, chopped
10 oz. peeled and deveined shrimp

1 lb. snow peas, topped and tailed
1/2 cup hoisin sauce
1 tbsp. fish sauce
1 tsp. coconut palm sugar or brown sugar
8 oz. mung bean sprouts
2 scallions, finely sliced

Heat a wok until a drop of water evaporates in a second or two. Add the pork belly and half the oil and stir-fry until crisp and brown. Remove to a plate, cover, and set aside. Drain excess fat from the wok.

Add the remaining oil to the wok, heat until just smoking, then add the ginger, garlic, and red onion. Stir-fry until fragrant and beginning to color. Add the shrimp and toss for 2 to 3 minutes, until the shrimp are just turning opaque. Add the snow peas, stir-fry for 1 minute then return the pork to the wok. Add the hoisin sauce, fish sauce, sugar, and bean sprouts and toss for 2 to 3 minutes until combined and hot. Sprinkle with scallions.

Serves 4

pork & lotus roots

see variations page 114

If lotus roots are unavailable, you can substitute any available root vegetable — potato, turnip, parsnip, carrot, sweet potato, or any combination of these. Wash or peel and slice your root vegetable, and stir-fry as directed until tender. Serve this dish with rice.

splash of vinegar
2 lotus roots
1 lb. pork fillet, sliced
3 tbsp. peanut or vegetable oil, divided
2 cloves garlic, finely chopped

1 oz. fresh ginger, finely chopped
1 bunch scallions, chopped
1/4 cup light soy sauce
2 tsp. chili sauce

Fill a large bowl with cold water and a good splash of vinegar. Peel the lotus roots and cut them into thin slices, placing each slice immediately into the bowl of vinegar water. Just before cooking, drain the lotus roots well and pat dry with a paper towel.

Heat a wok until a drop of water evaporates in a second or two. Add the pork and half the oil and stir-fry for 2 to 3 minutes, until just cooked. Transfer to a plate, cover and keep warm. Heat the remainder of the oil to just smoking and add the garlic, ginger, and scallions and stir-fry until fragrant and golden. Add the lotus root and cook, tossing occasionally, for 3 to 4 minutes, until it starts to change color and look translucent. Add the soy sauce and chili sauce and stir-fry for 1 to 2 minutes, until the lotus root begins to look caramelized. Return the pork and any juices to the wok. Toss well to combine and serve immediately.

Serves 4

beef & black beans

see variations page 115

Fermented black beans have a salty, pungent flavor that complements most meat and vegetables. If black beans are unavailable, substitute them, the water, and the cornstarch for 1/2 cup of good quality black bean sauce. Serve this dish with rice.

2 tbsp. peanut or vegetable oil
2 cloves garlic, finely chopped
1 yellow onion, halved lengthwise, and sliced
1 lb. beef sirloin, sliced
1/2 small cauliflower, cut into bite-size pieces
1 1/2 tbsp. salted and fermented black beans,
    mashed in 1/4 cup hot water

2 tbsp. light soy sauce
2 tsp. coconut palm sugar or brown sugar
2 tsp. cornstarch
1/4 cup cold water
1 small bunch fresh cilantro, chopped
additional cilantro leaves to garnish, if desired

Heat a wok until a drop of water evaporates in a second or two. Add the oil, garlic, and onion and stir until fragrant and golden. Add the beef and toss for 1 to 2 minutes, until it begins to color and cook.

Add the cauliflower to the wok and stir-fry for 1 to 2 minutes, until just starting to cook. Pour in the black beans in water, light soy sauce, and sugar and stir-fry for 2 to 3 minutes, until the cauliflower is tender. Mix the cornstarch and water, add to the wok, and stir immediately to prevent lumps from forming. Continue cooking for about 1 minute, until the sauce is thick and bubbling. Toss through half the cilantro. Sprinkle with the remaining cilantro and garnish with additional cilantro leaves, if desired.

Serves 4

beef with mixed peppers & soy

see variations page 116

The thinner ingredients are sliced for a stir-fry, the faster they will cook, but it is more important that they are sliced to a similar size so everything cooks evenly. Keep this in mind when preparing your ingredients. Serve this dish with rice or noodles.

1/4 cup light soy sauce
1 tbsp. sesame oil
1 tsp. coconut palm sugar or brown sugar
1 lb. beef sirloin, sliced
2 tbsp. peanut or vegetable oil
2 medium red onions, halved lengthwise,
    and sliced

2 cloves garlic, finely chopped
2 red bell peppers, sliced
1 green bell pepper, sliced
1 yellow bell pepper, sliced
2 tbsp. dark soy sauce

Put the light soy sauce, sesame oil, sugar, and beef into a bowl and mix well. Set aside for 10 minutes to marinate.

Heat a wok until a drop of water evaporates in a second or two. Add the peanut or vegetable oil, onion, and garlic and stir-fry until fragrant and beginning to color. Add the beef and marinade, and toss until just seared.

Add the bell peppers to the wok and toss for 2 to 3 minutes, until they have started to soften. Add the dark soy sauce and continue to stir-fry until the beef is just cooked and the peppers are tender. Serve immediately.

Serves 4

lamb with vietnamese mint & chile

see variations page 117

Vietnamese mint is also known as Vietnamese coriander, Cambodian mint, and laksa leaf. If it is unavailable, you can substitute cilantro, or regular mint, or a combination of the two herbs. Serve this dish with rice.

2 tbsp. peanut or vegetable oil
2 cloves garlic, finely chopped
1 oz. fresh ginger, finely chopped
2 long red chiles, seeded and finely sliced
1 large yellow onion, halved lengthwise, and sliced
1 lb. lamb fillet, sliced

1 lb. green beans, topped and tailed
1/4 cup light soy sauce
3 tbsp. sweet chili sauce
1 small bunch fresh Vietnamese mint, chopped (see Glossary, page 282)
1 red chile, sliced

Heat a wok until a drop of water evaporates in a second or two. Add the oil, garlic, ginger, long red chiles, and onion and stir-fry until fragrant and golden. Add the lamb and toss until it begins to color and cook.

Add the green beans and cook for 1 to 2 minutes, then add the light soy sauce and sweet chili sauce. Stir-fry until the beef is cooked through and the vegetables are crisp-tender. Toss through half the Vietnamese mint. Sprinkle with the remaining Vietnamese mint and extra red chile, and serve immediately.

Serves 4

mongolian-style lamb

see variations page 118

If the sauce for this lamb becomes too sticky and begins to burn while cooking, reduce the heat and add a little extra water, as required. Chinese cabbage is a versatile vegetable with pale green leaves and mild, sweet flavor. Serve this dish with rice.

2 tsp. cornstarch
3 tbsp. light soy sauce, divided
2 tsp. rice wine
2 cloves garlic, finely chopped
1 oz. fresh ginger, finely chopped
1 lb. lamb fillet, sliced
2 tbsp. peanut or vegetable oil

8 scallions, chopped
1/4 small Chinese cabbage, chopped
1 lb. snow peas, topped and tailed
3 tbsp. oyster sauce
2 tsp. sesame oil
1/4 cup water

Combine the cornstarch, 1 tablespoon light soy sauce, rice wine, garlic, and ginger in a bowl and mix well. Add the lamb and toss to coat. Set aside for 15 minutes to marinate.

Heat a wok until a drop of water evaporates in a second or two. Add the peanut or vegetable oil, scallions, and lamb and toss until the lamb starts to color and cook.

Add the Chinese cabbage and snow peas and cook for 1 to 2 minutes, then add the remaining 2 tablespoons light soy sauce, oyster sauce, sesame oil, and water. Continue stir-frying until the lamb is cooked through and the vegetables are crisp-tender. Serve immediately.

Serves 4

honey & sesame pork

see variations page 119

Try serving this delicious sweet and savory stir-fry with rice that has been steamed with ginger and a little sesame oil and then garnished with some finely sliced scallions.

2 tsp. sesame oil
1/4 cup light soy sauce, divided
1 oz. fresh ginger, finely chopped
1 lb. pork fillet, sliced
2 tbsp. peanut or vegetable oil
2 tbsp. sesame seeds
8 oz. mung bean sprouts

1 medium yellow onion, halved lengthwise,
    and sliced
8 oz. baby spinach
2 tbsp. honey
2 tsp. cornstarch
1/2 cup water

Put the sesame oil, 2 tablespoons light soy sauce, ginger, and pork into a bowl and mix well. Set aside for 10 minutes.

Heat a wok until a drop of water evaporates in a second or two. Add the peanut or vegetable oil and sesame seeds, tossing quickly to toast. Add the onion and stir-fry until fragrant and beginning to color. Add the pork and its marinade, tossing for 1 to 2 minutes, until the pork is just beginning to cook.

Add the bean sprouts, baby spinach, honey, and remaining 2 tablespoons light soy sauce to the wok. Quickly mix the cornstarch and water, add it to the wok, and stir immediately to prevent lumps from forming. Continue cooking for 1 to 2 minutes, until the sauce is thick and bubbling, tossing to coat the vegetables and meat. Serve immediately.

Serves 4

szechuan beans with pork

see variations page 120

Szechuan peppercorns have a hot, numbing flavor that is truly unique. Yardlong beans are a long, snakelike variety of stringless green bean that can be found in Asian grocery stores. If yardlong beans are unavailable, substitute regular stringless green beans.

peanut or vegetable oil for frying
1 1/2 lb. yardlong beans, cut into
   3-in. (7.5-cm.) lengths
2 tbsp. peanut or vegetable oil, for coating wok
2 tsp. Szechuan peppercorns
3 1/2 oz. ground pork

2 cloves garlic, finely chopped
1/2 oz. fresh ginger, finely chopped
4–8 dried red chiles, chopped
4 scallions, cut into bite-size pieces
1/4 cup light soy sauce

Pour peanut or vegetable oil into a large saucepan until it reaches a depth of 2 inches (5 cm.). Heat oil until the end of a wooden chopstick bubbles when dipped into the oil. Fry the yardlong beans in 3 batches, for 6 to 8 minutes each, until the beans are crinkly and developing brown spots. Remove from the saucepan using a slotted spoon and drain on paper towels. Remove the oil from the heat.

Heat a wok until a drop of water evaporates in a second or two. Add 2 tablespoons oil to the wok followed by the Szechuan peppercorns; stir-fry for 10 seconds then add the ground pork and stir, breaking up any lumps, until the pork is cooked and beginning to crisp. Add the garlic, ginger, dried chiles, and scallions and stir-fry until fragrant and beginning to color. Add the yardlong beans to the wok, then add the soy sauce, and stir-fry for 1 to 2 minutes more, until the beans are hot and everything is well mixed. Serve immediately.

Serves 4

teriyaki pork

see variations page 121

The sauce in this recipe provides the dark, sticky, savory flavors loved by fans of teriyaki. Try doubling the recipe and storing some in the refrigerator for later use in stir-fries or to baste meat. Serve this dish with rice.

2 tbsp. light soy sauce
1 tbsp. dark soy sauce
1 tbsp. brown sugar
1 tbsp. honey
1/2 oz. fresh ginger, finely chopped

1 clove garlic, finely chopped
1/2 cup water, divided
2 tsp. cornstarch
2 tbsp. peanut or vegetable oil
1 medium red onion, halved lengthwise, and chopped

1 lb. pork fillet, sliced
1 large broccoli, cut into bite-size florets
2 medium zucchini, halved lengthwise and sliced

Put the light soy sauce, dark soy sauce, brown sugar, honey, ginger, garlic, and 1/4 cup water into a saucepan over medium heat, bring to a boil, and simmer for 2 to 3 minutes, until the sugar has dissolved. Quickly mix the cornstarch with the remaining 1/4 cup water, add it to the pan, and stir immediately to prevent lumps from forming. Cook the sauce for about 30 seconds, until it is thick and bubbling. Remove from the heat and set aside.

Heat a wok until a drop of water evaporates in a second or two. Add the oil, onion, and pork, and stir-fry for 1 to 2 minutes, until the onion begins to color and the pork is partly cooked. Add the broccoli and toss for 1 to 2 minutes more. Add the zucchini and toss for 1 minute before adding the teriyaki sauce. Stir-fry until all the ingredients are coated in sauce, the vegetables are crisp-tender, and the pork is cooked. Serve immediately.

Serves 4

ginger beef with shitake mushrooms

see base recipe page 67

ginger beef with green bell peppers
Omit the shitake mushrooms. Add 2 large green bell peppers, sliced, to the wok with the red bell pepper. Complete the recipe as directed, adding a little beef broth in place of the mushroom liquid, if required.

ginger pork with green beans
Substitute 1 pound thinly sliced pork fillet for the beef, and 1 pound of topped and tailed green beans for the shitake mushrooms. Add a little vegetable broth to the wok in place of the mushroom liquid, if required.

ginger beef with button mushrooms
Substitute 1 pound sliced button mushrooms for the shitake mushrooms. Add a little beef broth in place of the mushroom liquid, if required.

ginger beef with chili & onions
Omit the shitake mushrooms. Increase the onions to 2 large yellow onions, sliced, and add them to the wok with 2 seeded and finely sliced red chiles. Add a little extra beef broth to the wok in place of the reserved mushroom liquid, if required.

ground pork with lemongrass

see base recipe page 68

ground pork with lime & chile
Substitute 2 seeded and finely sliced red chiles for the lemongrass. Complete the recipe as directed, adding the zest and juice of 1 lime to the wok with the soy sauce, and increasing the sugar to 1 tablespoon. Serve with lime wedges.

ground beef with lemongrass
Prepare the basic recipe, but substitute 1 pound ground beef for the pork.

ground lamb with lemongrass & vietnamese mint
Substitute 1 pound ground lamb for the pork. Complete the recipe as directed, adding a bunch chopped fresh Vietnamese mint to the stir-fry just before serving.

ground pork with lemongrass & ginger
Increase the fresh ginger to 1 1/2 ounces, peeled and cut into matchsticks.

lamb with thai basil

see base recipe page 70

lamb with thai basil & chili
Add 2 seeded and finely sliced red chiles to the wok with the ginger, garlic, lemongrass, and scallions. Serve the stir-fry with 1 finely sliced red chile.

beef with thai basil
Prepare the basic recipe, but substitute 1 pound thinly sliced beef sirloin for the lamb.

pork with thai basil
Prepare the basic recipe, but substitute 1 pound thinly sliced pork fillet for the lamb.

lamb with thai basil & ginger
Increase the fresh ginger to 1 1/2 ounces, peeled and cut into matchsticks.

variations

red curry lamb & eggplant

see base recipe page 72

green curry lamb & eggplant
Prepare the basic recipe, but substitute 1 seeded and finely sliced green chile for the red chile, and 2 tablespoons green curry paste for the red curry paste.

red curry lamb & squash
Prepare the basic recipe, but substitute 1/2 small butternut squash, sliced, for the eggplant.

red curry beef & eggplant
Prepare the basic recipe, but substitute 1 pound sliced beef fillet for the lamb.

red curry lamb & lotus root
Substitute 1 to 2 lotus roots for the eggplant. Peel and slice the lotus roots and put the slices into a bowl of cold water with a splash of vinegar. Just before cooking, drain the lotus root and pat dry with paper towels. Add the lotus root to the wok in place of the eggplant and complete the recipe as directed.

sticky pork with chinese broccoli

see base recipe page 73

sticky beef with chinese broccoli
Prepare the basic recipe, but substitute 1 pound sliced beef sirloin for the pork.

sticky pork with bok choy
Prepare the basic recipe, but substitute 8 baby bok choy, cut into bite-size pieces, for the Chinese broccoli.

sticky lamb with chinese cabbage
Substitute 1 pound sliced lamb fillet for the pork and 1/2 a small chopped Chinese cabbage for the Chinese broccoli and complete the recipe as directed.

sticky pork with mushrooms
Omit the Chinese broccoli. Add 1 pound sliced mushrooms to the wok with the scallions. Stir-fry until the mushrooms start to color and soften before adding the pork. Fry until the pork is cooked, adding a little water if needed, and serve immediately.

variations

crispy beef

see base recipe page 74

crispy pork
Prepare the basic recipe, but substitute 1 pound finely sliced pork fillet for the beef.

crispy beef with noodles
Prepare 12 ounces of fresh egg noodles according to package directions. Add the noodles to the wok with the beef and bok choy, and stir-fry until the beef and noodles are hot and the bok choy is wilted. There is no need to serve this variation with rice.

crispy lamb
Prepare the basic recipe, but substitute 1 pound finely sliced lamb fillet for the beef.

crispy chili beef
Prepare the basic recipe, but increase the red chiles to 3 to 4, to taste, and add 2 to 3 teaspoons of sambal oelek, to taste, to the wok with the sauces.

beef with red chili paste

see base recipe page 76

beef with shrimp paste
Omit the chili paste. Combine 2 teaspoons shrimp paste, 1 clove peeled and finely chopped garlic, 2 tablespoons rice wine, and 1 seeded and finely sliced red chile in a bowl. Add the beef and set aside for 15 minutes to marinate. Complete the recipe as directed.

pork with red chili paste
Prepare the basic recipe, but substitute 1 pound sliced pork fillet for the beef.

beef with red chili paste & peanuts
Add 1/2 cup chopped, roasted peanuts to the wok with the bok choy. Serve garnished with extra chopped, roasted peanuts.

beef with red chili paste & thai basil
Prepare the basic recipe, but add 1/2 bunch fresh chopped Thai basil to the wok just before serving. Garnish the finished stir-fry with another 1/2 bunch fresh Thai basil leaves.

variations

sweet & sour pork

see base recipe page 78

sweet & sour pork with noodles
Prepare 1 pound of fresh egg noodles according to package directions and add to the wok with the snow peas. Complete the recipe as directed. There is no need to serve this variation with rice.

sweet & sour beef
Prepare the basic recipe, but substitute 1 pound sliced beef sirloin for the pork.

sweet & sour pork & shrimp
Add 8 ounces small, cooked shrimp to the wok with the pineapple and snow peas. Cook until everything is heated through.

sweet & sour pork with asian greens
Substitute 1 bunch Chinese broccoli, cut into bite-size pieces, for the carrots and peppers. Complete the recipe as directed, adding a 1/4 small, shredded Chinese cabbage and 4 chopped baby bok choy to the wok with the snow peas.

variations

lamb & squash with green chile & lime

see base recipe page 80

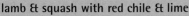

lamb & squash with red chile & lime
Prepare the basic recipe, but substitute 2 seeded and sliced long red chiles for the green chiles. Garnish the stir-fry with a sliced red chile as well as the cilantro.

beef & squash with green chile & lime
Prepare the basic recipe, but substitute 1 pound sliced beef fillet for the lamb.

pork & green bell peppers with black pepper & lime
Substitute 1 to 2 teaspoons crushed black peppercorns to the wok for the chiles; 1 pound sliced pork fillet for the lamb; and 2 large green bell peppers, cored and sliced, for the yellow squash.

lamb & squash with coconut & lime
Reduce the green chile to 1, and omit the kecap manis. Add 1/2 cup coconut milk to the wok with the soy sauce, and garnish the finished stir-fry with 2 tablespoons toasted shredded coconut.

beef with bamboo shoots & baby corn

see base recipe page 81

pork with bamboo shoots & baby corn
Prepare the basic recipe, but substitute 1 pound sliced pork fillet for the beef.

beef with asparagus & baby corn
Prepare the basic recipe, but substitute 2 bunches sliced asparagus for the bamboo shoots.

beef with bamboo shoots & mushrooms
Omit the baby corn. Add 10 ounces sliced mushrooms to the wok after the beef, stir-frying until softened, before completing the recipe as directed.

beef with bamboo shoots & snow peas
Prepare the basic recipe, but substitute 8 ounces topped and tailed snow peas for the baby corn.

variations

ground lamb & water chestnuts in hoisin sauce

see base recipe page 82

ground beef & water chestnuts in hoisin sauce
Prepare the basic recipe, but substitute 1 pound ground beef for the lamb.

ground pork & water chestnuts in hoisin sauce
Prepare the basic recipe, but substitute 1 pound ground pork for the lamb.

ground lamb & water chestnuts in oyster sauce
Prepare the basic recipe, but substitute 1/2 cup oyster sauce for the hoisin sauce.

ground pork & apple in hoisin sauce
Substitute 3 green apples, peeled, cored, and chopped, for the water chestnuts. Complete the recipe as directed, taking care not to overcook the apples.

chile & basil beef with peanuts

see base recipe page 84

chile & basil lamb with peanuts
Prepare the basic recipe, but substitute 1 pound sliced lamb fillet for the beef.

chile & basil beef with cashews
Substitute 2/3 cup chopped roasted cashews for the peanuts.

chile & cilantro beef with peanuts
Substitute 1 bunch chopped fresh cilantro for the basil.

chile & basil pork with almonds
Prepare the basic recipe, but substitute 1 pound sliced pork fillet for the beef and 2/3 cup chopped roasted almonds for the peanuts.

pork belly & shrimp with ginger & garlic

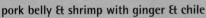

see base recipe page 86

pork belly & shrimp with ginger & chile
Reduce the garlic to 2 cloves, finely chopped, and add 2 seeded and finely sliced red chiles to the wok with the ginger, garlic, and red onion.

pork belly & fish cakes with ginger & garlic
Prepare the basic recipe, but substitute 10 ounces sliced fish cakes for the shrimp.

pork belly & shrimp with plum sauce
Substitute 1/2 cup plum sauce for the hoisin sauce and 2 tablespoons light soy sauce for the fish sauce. Complete the recipe as directed.

beef & shrimp with ginger & garlic
Substitute 10 ounces sliced beef sirloin for the pork belly. Stir-fry the beef until just cooked and tender before removing to a plate to keep warm. Complete the recipe as directed, returning the beef to the wok with the sauces.

variations

pork & lotus roots

see base recipe page 88

pork & lotus roots with chiles
Add 2 seeded and finely chopped red chiles to the wok with the garlic, ginger, and scallions and increase the chili sauce to 1 to 2 tablespoons, to taste.

pork & asian greens
Omit the lotus roots. Add 1 large bunch chopped Chinese flowering cauliflower to the wok following the scallions and stir-fry for 1 to 2 minutes. Add 8 baby bok choy, quartered, to the wok with the soy sauce.

beef & lotus roots
Prepare the basic recipe, but substitute 1 pound sliced beef sirloin for the pork.

pork & turnips
Prepare the basic recipe, but substitute 2 peeled and thinly sliced turnips for the lotus root.

pork & onion with ginger
Omit the lotus roots. Increase the fresh ginger to 1 1/2 ounces, finely chopped, and add 2 yellow onions, halved and sliced, to the wok with the garlic, ginger, and scallions. Complete the recipe as directed, adding 4 chopped baby bok choy to the wok with the sauces.

variations

beef & black beans

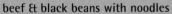

see base recipe page 90

beef & black beans with noodles
Prepare 1 pound of egg noodles according to package directions and add to the wok with the black beans. Complete the recipe as directed. There is no need to serve this variation with rice.

pork & black beans
Prepare the basic recipe, but substitute 1 pound sliced pork fillet for the beef.

beef & black beans with red bell peppers
Prepare the basic recipe, but substitute 2 sliced large red bell peppers for the cauliflower.

lamb & black beans
Prepare the basic recipe, but substitute 1 pound sliced lamb fillet for the beef.

variations

beef with mixed peppers & soy

see base recipe page 92

lamb with mixed peppers & soy
Prepare the basic recipe, but substitute 1 pound sliced lamb fillet for the beef.

beef with mushroom & soy
Substitute 8 ounces sliced button mushrooms, 2 large, sliced portobello mushrooms, and 8 ounces sliced shitake mushrooms for the peppers. Complete the recipe as directed.

pork with mixed peppers & soy
Prepare the basic recipe, but substitute 1 pound sliced pork fillet for the beef.

beef with broccoli & soy
Substitute 2 large heads broccoli, cut into bite-size florets, for the peppers.

lamb with vietnamese mint & chile

see base recipe page 94

lamb with basil & chile
Substitute 1 small bunch fresh basil, chopped, for the Vietnamese mint.

lamb with vietnamese mint & peanuts
Prepare the basic recipe, but omit the red chiles and add 2/3 cup roasted, chopped peanuts
to the wok just before serving.

beef with vietnamese mint & chile
Prepare the basic recipe, but substitute 1 pound sliced beef sirloin for the lamb.

lamb with cilantro & szechuan peppers
Omit the Vietnamese mint and red chiles. Add 2 teaspoons crushed Szechuan peppercorns
to the wok just before the garlic, ginger, and onion. Complete the recipe as directed,
substituting 1 small bunch fresh cilantro, chopped, for the Vietnamese mint.

variations

mongolian-style lamb

see base recipe page 96

mongolian-style beef
Prepare the basic recipe, but substitute 1 pound sliced beef sirloin for the lamb.

mongolian-style lamb & zucchini
Prepare the basic recipe, but substitute 2 zucchinis, halved lengthwise and thinly sliced, for the snow peas.

mongolian-style lamb with noodles
Prepare 12 ounces of egg noodles according to package directions and add to the wok with the snow peas. Complete the recipe as directed. There is no need to serve this variation with rice.

mongolian-style lamb with carrots
Substitute 2 large carrots, halved lengthwise and thinly sliced, for the Chinese cabbage.

honey & sesame pork

see base recipe page 97

honey & sesame lamb
Prepare the basic recipe, but substitute 1 pound sliced lamb fillet for the pork.

honey & lemon pork
Omit the sesame seeds and reduce the sesame oil to 1 teaspoon. Add the zest and juice of 1 lemon to the marinade. Complete the recipe as directed.

honey & sesame pork with chile
Prepare the basic recipe, but add 2 seeded and finely sliced red chiles to the wok with the onion.

honey & sesame pork with noodles
Prepare 12 ounces of fresh udon noodles according to package directions and add to the wok with the bean sprouts and baby spinach. Complete the recipe as directed. There is no need to serve this variation with rice.

sweet chili & sesame pork
Substitute 1/4 cup sweet chili sauce for the honey and final 2 tablespoons light soy sauce.

variations

szechuan beans with pork

see base recipe page 98

chili beans with pork
Prepare the basic recipe, but omit the Szechuan peppercorns. Replace half the dried chiles for 2 to 4 finely sliced fresh red chiles. For an extra kick, add 1 to 2 teaspoons red chili paste to the wok with the soy sauce.

szechuan green beans with pork
Prepare the basic recipe, but substitute 1 1/2 pounds stringless green beans, topped and tailed, for the yardlong beans.

garlic & ginger beans with pork
Omit the Szechuan peppercorns and dried chiles. Increase the garlic to 4 cloves, peeled and finely chopped, and the fresh ginger to 1 1/2 ounces, peeled and finely chopped.

peanut szechuan beans with pork
Crush 1 cup peanuts using a mortar and pestle and add to the wok with the garlic, ginger, and scallions. Complete the recipe as directed.

variations

teriyaki pork

see base recipe page 100

teriyaki beef
Prepare the basic recipe, but substitute 1 pound sliced beef fillet for the pork.

teriyaki pork noodles
Prepare 12 ounces of fresh udon noodles according to package directions and add to the wok with the zucchini. Complete the recipe as directed. There is no need to serve this variation with rice.

teriyaki lamb
Prepare the basic recipe, but substitute 1 pound sliced lamb fillet for the pork.

spicy teriyaki pork
Add 1 to 2 tablespoons chili sauce, to taste, to the saucepan with the light and dark soy sauces and 1 seeded and finely sliced red chile to the wok with the onion and pork.

vegetable & tofu

Vegetables make up an integral part of most stir-fry dishes and provide a delicious range of flavors, textures, and colors. There are many exciting Asian varieties to experiment with, and many greens can be easily interchanged. There are also many varieties of bean curd products, such as the different types of tofu and tempeh, that provide texture and carry flavor well.

broccoli & black bean

see variations page 155

Fermented black beans should be available in a package from an Asian grocer. If you cannot find fermented black beans, simply replace them, the water, and the cornstarch with 2/3 to 3/4 cup of commercially prepared black bean sauce. Serve this dish with rice.

2 tbsp. peanut or vegetable oil
2 cloves garlic, finely chopped
1 red onion, halved lengthwise, and chopped
2 large heads broccoli, cut into bite-size florets
1 tbsp. salted and fermented black beans, mashed in
    1/4 cup hot water

2 tbsp. light soy sauce
2 tsp. cornstarch
1/2 cup cold water
1 small bunch fresh cilantro, chopped

Heat a wok until a drop of water evaporates in a second or two. Add the oil, garlic, and red onion and stir until fragrant and golden. Add the broccoli and toss for 1 to 2 minutes. Pour in the black beans in water and soy sauce and stir-fry for 2 to 3 minutes more, until the broccoli is tender.

Mix the cornstarch and water, add to the wok and stir immediately to prevent lumps from forming. Continue cooking the sauce for 1 to 2 minutes, until it is thick and bubbling, then toss through half the cilantro. Sprinkle with the remaining cilantro.

Serves 4

chile–eggplant

see variations page 156

Eggplant is well suited to stir-frying, because it is delicious slightly charred and smoky and it absorbs flavor. If the wok seems overloaded, try adding the eggplant in two batches, removing one while you stir-fry the other and adding them back together at the end. Serve with steamed greens, rice, and extra sweet chili sauce on the side.

3 tbsp. peanut or vegetable oil
2 long red chiles, seeded and finely sliced
2 cloves garlic, finely chopped
4 scallions, cut into bite-size pieces
2 large eggplant, halved lengthwise and sliced
    into strips

1 tbsp. miso paste (see Glossary, page 281)
3 tbsp. light soy sauce
3 tbsp. sweet chili sauce
3 tbsp. water

Heat a wok until a drop of water evaporates in a second or two. Add the oil, chiles, garlic, and scallions and stir-fry until fragrant and golden. Add the eggplant and toss for 2 to 3 minutes, until the eggplant is golden.

Stir in the miso paste, soy sauce, sweet chili sauce, and water and stir-fry for 2 to 3 minutes more, until the eggplant has softened and absorbed the juices.

Serves 4

eggplant, tofu & tomato

see variations page 157

The tomatoes added toward the end of this stir-fry help to create a sauce as they soften; adding a little water can help this process if the mixture still seems a little dry. Serve on a bed of steamed rice.

1 (12-oz.) package extra-firm tofu
3 tbsp. peanut or vegetable oil
1 oz. fresh ginger, finely chopped
2 cloves garlic, finely chopped
1 yellow onion, halved lengthwise and chopped

1 large eggplant, halved lengthwise and sliced
1/4 cup light soy sauce
3 large tomatoes, cored and cut into
    bite-size pieces
1 small bunch fresh Thai basil, chopped

Rinse, drain, and pat the tofu dry with paper towels, then slice it into bite-size pieces. Heat a wok until a drop of water evaporates in a second or two. Add the oil, fresh ginger, garlic, and onion and stir-fry until fragrant and golden. Add the eggplant and toss for 1 to 2 minutes, until it starts to color and soften, then add the tofu.

Stir-fry the tofu and eggplant for 2 to 3 minutes before adding the soy sauce and tomatoes. Toss for 1 to 2 minutes more, until the tomatoes are heated through and beginning to soften. Toss through half the Thai basil. Sprinkle with the remaining Thai basil.

Serves 4

ginger, tofu & asian greens

see variations page 158

Ginger is wonderful for livening up the flavors of milder ingredients such as tofu. The Asian greens in this recipe can be exchanged for another leafy vegetable if you have trouble finding them. When using scallions, reserve the tops of the green stems, and finely slice them diagonally to use as a garnish on your dish. Serve this dish with rice.

1 (12-oz.) package extra-firm tofu
2 tbsp. peanut or vegetable oil
1 1/2 oz. fresh ginger, finely chopped
2 cloves garlic, finely chopped
4 scallions, cut into bite-size pieces

2 tsp. coconut palm sugar or brown sugar
1/4 cup light soy sauce
4 baby bok choy, quartered lengthwise
1/4 small Chinese cabbage, shredded

Rinse, drain, and pat the tofu dry with paper towels before cutting it into bite-size pieces. Heat a wok until a drop of water evaporates in a second or two. Add the oil, fresh ginger, garlic, and scallions and stir-fry until fragrant and golden. Add the tofu and toss for 1 to 2 minutes. Stir in the sugar and soy sauce and stir-fry for 2 to 3 minutes more.

Add the bok choy and Chinese cabbage and stir-fry for 1 to 2 minutes, until they are coated in sauce and beginning to wilt. Serve immediately.

Serves 4

green vegetables with sesame

see variations page 159

Sesame oil adds a delicious, nutty flavor to stir-fries, but keep in mind that it has a very low smoke point, so it should be used as a seasoning rather than a cooking oil. Serve this dish with rice.

3 tbsp. peanut or vegetable oil
3 tbsp. sesame seeds, divided
2 cloves garlic, finely chopped
1 head broccoli, cut into bite-size florets
1 medium zucchini, halved lengthwise and
    thinly sliced

1 lb. green beans, topped and tailed
8 oz. tatsoi leaves (see Glossary, page 280)
2 tbsp. dark soy sauce
3 tbsp. light soy sauce
1 tbsp. sesame oil

Heat a wok until a drop of water evaporates in a second or two. Add the oil, 2 tablespoons of the sesame seeds, and garlic and stir-fry until fragrant and golden. Add the broccoli and green beans and stir-fry for 2 to 3 minutes more before adding the zucchini.

Toss for 1 to 2 minutes, then add the tatsoi, both soy sauces, and the sesame oil, stirring to coat all the ingredients with the sauce. Once the vegetables are crisp-tender and the tatsoi wilted, garnish with the remaining 1 tablespoon sesame seeds and serve.

Serves 4

tempeh & green vegetables

see variations page 160

Tempeh is a traditional Indonesian food. This fermented soy bean product can be found in most grocery stores, but if unavailable, it can be easily substituted for an equal quantity of extra-firm tofu. Serve this dish with rice.

2 tbsp. peanut or vegetable oil
1 stalk lemongrass, outer leaves and root
    discarded, white part finely chopped
2 cloves garlic, finely chopped
1 (12-oz.) package tempeh, sliced into
    bite-size pieces
1 head broccoli, cut into bite-size florets

1 lb. green beans, topped and tailed
1 medium zucchini, halved lengthwise and
    thinly sliced
1/3 cup sweet chili sauce
2 tbsp. light soy sauce
1 small bunch fresh cilantro, roughly chopped

Heat a wok until a drop of water evaporates in a second or two. Add the oil, lemongrass, and garlic and stir-fry until fragrant and golden. Add the tempeh and toss for 1 to 2 minutes, until the tempeh is lightly golden.

Add the broccoli and green beans and stir-fry for 2 to 3 minutes more before adding the zucchini. Toss for 1 to 2 minutes, and then add the sweet chili and soy sauces, tossing to coat all the ingredients with the sauce. Once the vegetables are crisp-tender, toss through half the cilantro. Sprinkle with the remaining cilantro.

Serves 4

sweet chili & vegetables

see variations page 161

Sweet chili sauce has a balance of sweet, salty, and sour flavors, with a little heat from the chile. It is generally fairly mild, and is perfect for chili beginners. The water chestnuts add crunch and a nutty flavor to this dish. Serve this dish with noodles.

2 tbsp. peanut or vegetable oil
1 long red chile, seeded and finely sliced
2 cloves garlic, finely chopped
1 medium yellow onion, halved lengthwise
    and chopped
8 oz. button mushrooms, sliced
1 large red bell pepper, cut into bite-size pieces

1 bunch of broccolini, cut into bite-size pieces
4 oz. baby spinach
1 (8-oz.) can sliced water chestnuts, drained
1/2 cup sweet chili sauce
1 tbsp. light soy sauce
1 small bunch fresh flat-leaf parsley, chopped

Heat a wok until a drop of water evaporates in a second or two. Add the oil, chile, garlic, and onion and stir-fry until fragrant and golden. Add the mushrooms and bell pepper and stir-fry for 2 to 3 minutes, until the mushrooms and peppers soften.

Add the broccolini to the wok and toss for 1 to 2 minutes, then add the baby spinach, water chestnuts, sweet chili sauce, and soy sauce, tossing to coat all the ingredients with the sauce. Once the vegetables are crisp-tender and the spinach wilted, toss through half the parsley. Sprinkle with the remaining parsley and serve.

Serves 4

mixed mushrooms

see variations page 162

Asian grocers usually stock a wide range of fresh, canned, and dried mushrooms, but if you can't find a particular variety, simply substitute it for a similar amount of another. If using dried mushrooms, reconstitute them in hot water before measuring them for this recipe. Serve this dish with rice.

3 tbsp. peanut or vegetable oil
2 cloves garlic, finely chopped
4 scallions, cut into bite-size pieces
5 oz. button mushrooms, sliced
5 oz. oyster mushrooms, halved

5 oz. fresh shitake mushrooms, sliced
1 (15-oz.) can straw mushrooms, drained
1/4 cup oyster sauce
2 tbsp. light soy sauce

Heat a wok until a drop of water evaporates in a second or two. Add the oil, garlic, and scallions and stir-fry until fragrant and golden. Add the button, oyster, and shitake mushrooms and toss for 2 to 3 minutes, until the mushrooms color and soften.

Add the straw mushrooms, oyster sauce, and soy sauce and stir-fry for a few minutes, until the straw mushrooms are heated through and everything is coated in sauce. Serve immediately.

Serves 4

asian greens & oyster sauce

see variations page 163

Many markets and grocers offer a fantastic range of Asian leafy greens, and they can be used interchangeably. Just be sure to add those with thicker stems to the wok first, even slicing very thick stems in half, because they will take longer to cook. Reserve the thinner, smaller leaves for last, because they cook as quickly as they heat. Serve this dish with rice.

2 tbsp. peanut or vegetable oil
1/2 oz. fresh ginger, finely chopped
1 bunch Chinese broccoli, cut into
    3-in. (7.5-cm.) lengths
6 baby bok choy, quartered lengthwise

1/4 small Chinese cabbage, torn into
    bite-size pieces
1/2 cup oyster sauce

Heat a wok until a drop of water evaporates in a second or two. Add the oil and ginger and stir-fry until fragrant and golden. Add the Chinese broccoli and toss for 1 to 2 minutes before adding the bok choy. Stir-fry for 1 to 2 minutes more before adding the Chinese cabbage and oyster sauce, tossing for 1 to 2 minutes, until the greens are coated in sauce and beginning to wilt. Serve immediately.

Serves 4

celery & red onion with black pepper & lime

see variations page 164

Stir-frying the celery until it is tender, but still crisp, makes this dish a delicious, textural accompaniment to any meat, or a stand–alone meal with rice.

zest and juice of 1 lime
1/4 cup light soy sauce
1 tbsp. coconut palm sugar or brown sugar
2 tbsp. peanut or vegetable oil
2 cloves garlic, finely chopped
1 tsp. freshly ground black pepper

2 large red onions, halved lengthwise and sliced
1/2 large head celery, sliced
1 tsp. cornstarch
1/4 cup cold water
1 small bunch fresh Vietnamese mint, chopped
(see Glossary, page 282)

Combine the lime zest and juice, light soy sauce, and sugar in a bowl, and stir to dissolve the sugar. Set aside.

Heat a wok until a drop of water evaporates in a second or two. Add the oil, garlic, black pepper, and red onion and stir-fry until fragrant and golden. Add the celery and toss for 1 to 2 minutes. Add the lime-soy sauce mixture and toss until the celery is just tender.

Mix the cornstarch and water, add it to the wok, and stir immediately to prevent lumps from forming. Continue cooking for 1 to 2 minutes, until the sauce is thick and bubbling. Toss through half the Vietnamese mint. Sprinkle with the remaining mint and serve.

Serves 4

seasoned lettuce

see variations page 165

Although it may seem odd, iceberg lettuce makes a fantastic stir-fry ingredient; it cooks extremely quickly and takes on other flavors easily. Cook it until it has softened around the edges, but still has a little crispness. Try this stir-fry as an accompaniment to meat and rice dishes.

1 tbsp. light soy sauce
1 tbsp. kecap manis
2 tsp. sesame oil
2 tsp. rice wine
1 tsp. coconut palm sugar or brown sugar

1 large head iceberg lettuce
2 tbsp. peanut or vegetable oil
1/2 oz. fresh ginger, finely chopped
2 cloves garlic, finely chopped
4 scallions, cut into bite-size pieces

Combine the soy sauce, kecap manis, sesame oil, rice wine, and sugar in a small bowl and stir until the sugar dissolves. Set aside. Remove the outer leaves and the core of the iceberg lettuce and discard. Tear the leaves into large chunks, about 3 inches (7.5 cm.).

Heat a wok until a drop of water evaporates in a second or two. Add the peanut or vegetable oil, ginger, garlic, and scallions and stir until fragrant and golden.

Add the iceberg lettuce and toss for 1 minute, until it just starts to soften, before adding the soy sauce mixture. Stir-fry for another minute, until the lettuce is coated in sauce and beginning to wilt. Serve immediately.

Serves 4

tofu with green chili paste

see variations page 166

Pastes feature often in Asian cooking as they are a great way to add a big boost of flavor, and there are many available ready-made in stores, including curry, shrimp, tamarind, and chili pastes. Some are easy to make, but good quality ones can be purchased to save time. Serve this dish with rice.

3 long green chiles, halved, seeded, and chopped
1 oz. fresh ginger, chopped
1 clove garlic, chopped
1/2 tsp. salt
1/2 tsp. pepper
1 tbsp. sesame oil
1 tbsp. lemon juice

1 tsp. coconut palm sugar or brown sugar
1 (12-oz.) package extra-firm tofu
2 tbsp. peanut or vegetable oil
1 large yellow onion, halved lengthwise, and chopped
3 tbsp. light soy sauce
8 baby bok choy, cut into bite-size pieces
2–3 tbsp. water

Put the green chiles, ginger, garlic, salt, and pepper into a mortar and pestle and pound to a rough paste. Add the sesame oil and pound again until the paste is smoother, before mixing in the lemon juice and sugar. Transfer the paste to a small bowl and set aside. Rinse, drain, and pat the tofu dry on paper towels before cutting it into bite-size pieces.

Heat a wok until a drop of water evaporates in a second or two. Add the peanut or vegetable oil and onion and stir-fry until fragrant and golden. Add the tofu and toss for 1 to 2 minutes. Add the chili paste and stir-fry until the tofu is coated and the paste is fragrant and beginning to color. Add the soy sauce and bok choy and stir-fry for 1 to 2 minutes, adding a little water if needed, until the bok choy is beginning to wilt. Serve immediately.

Serves 4

garlic & pepper tofu

see variations page 167

Tofu is an excellent way to add protein to vegetarian dishes. While this recipe calls for extra firm, most types of tofu, excluding silken, could be used in its place; just take extra care when stir-frying, because softer ones will break up more easily. Serve with rice.

1 (12-oz.) package extra-firm tofu
3 tbsp. peanut or vegetable oil
4 cloves garlic, finely chopped
1 yellow onion, halved lengthwise, and sliced
1 large red bell pepper, sliced

1 large green bell pepper, sliced
2 tbsp. light soy sauce
1 tbsp. dark soy sauce
1 tsp. freshly ground black pepper
2–3 tbsp. water

Rinse, drain, and pat the tofu dry with paper towels, then cut it into bite-size pieces.

Heat a wok until a drop of water evaporates in a second or two. Add the oil, garlic, and onion and stir-fry until fragrant and golden. Add the bell peppers and toss for 1 to 2 minutes, until they start to soften, then add the tofu and stir-fry for 2 to 3 minutes.

Add the soy sauces and black pepper and toss for 1 to 2 minutes more, adding a little water if needed, until the tofu is heated through and the peppers are crisp-tender.

Serves 4

squash & peanuts

see variations page 168

Butternut squash is perfect for stir-frying, because it caramelizes, giving sweetness to the dish. Any variety of pumpkin could be used in place of the butternut in this recipe. Serve this dish with rice.

1/3 cup peanut butter	2 tbsp. peanut or vegetable oil
2/3 cup water	1 oz. fresh ginger, finely chopped
1 tbsp. dark soy sauce	2 cloves garlic, finely chopped
1 tbsp. sweet chili sauce	1 medium red onion, sliced
1 tbsp. sesame oil	2–3 tbsp. water, if needed
1 tsp. chili sauce	1/2 cup roasted peanuts, chopped
1 medium butternut squash	1 small bunch fresh cilantro, roughly chopped

Put the peanut butter, water, dark soy sauce, sweet chili sauce, sesame oil, and chili sauce into a small bowl and whisk to combine. Set aside. Cut the butternut squash in half lengthwise, peel, seed, and slice each half into 1/2-inch (1.25-cm.) slices.

Heat a wok until a drop of water evaporates in a second or two. Add the peanut or vegetable oil, ginger, garlic, and red onion and stir-fry until fragrant and golden. Add the butternut squash and stir-fry for 5 to 6 minutes, until the squash is starting to soften and color.

Add the peanut butter mixture and stir-fry for 4 to 5 minutes, until the squash is tender. Reduce the heat, adding a little water if needed. Toss the peanuts and half the cilantro through the stir-fry. Sprinkle with the remaining cilantro and serve immediately.

Serves 4

cashews & mixed vegetables

see variations page 169

Nuts are a delicious addition to stir-fries, adding extra texture and flavor. Cashews and peanuts are a common addition, but almonds, walnuts, or even seeds such as pepitas, work just as well.

2 tbsp. peanut or vegetable oil
1 long green chile, seeded and finely sliced
2 cloves garlic, finely chopped
1 medium yellow onion, halved lengthwise,
    and chopped
8 oz. button mushrooms, sliced
1 large red bell pepper, cut into bite-size pieces

1 head broccoli, cut into bite-size florets
4 baby bok choy, quartered
1 (8-oz.) can baby corn, drained and sliced
3 tbsp. light soy sauce
2 tsp. cornstarch
1/2 cup cold water
2/3 cup roasted cashews, chopped

Heat a wok until a drop of water evaporates in a second or two. Add the oil, chile, garlic, and onion and stir-fry until fragrant and golden. Add the mushrooms and bell pepper and stir-fry for 2 to 3 minutes.

Add the broccoli to the wok and toss for 1 to 2 minutes. Add the bok choy, baby corn, and soy sauce, tossing all until the bok choy begins to wilt. Mix the cornstarch and water, add it to the wok, and stir immediately to prevent lumps from forming. Continue cooking until the sauce is thick and bubbly, about 1 to 2 minutes. Toss through half the roasted cashews. Sprinkle with the remaining cashews and serve.

Serves 4

marinated tofu

see variations page 170

While quite mild tasting on its own, tofu absorbs flavors like a sponge, making it the perfect partner for the strong tastes of Asian cuisine. In as little as 5 minutes, the tofu will take on the flavors of whatever it is marinated in. Serve this dish with rice.

2 cloves garlic, finely chopped
1/4 cup light soy sauce
1 tsp. coconut palm sugar or brown sugar
2 tsp. rice wine

1 lb. extra-firm tofu
2 tbsp. peanut or vegetable oil
1 large red onion, peeled and chopped
8 oz. tatsoi leaves (see Glossary, page 280)

Combine the garlic, soy sauce, sugar, and rice wine in a bowl. Rinse, drain, and pat the tofu dry with paper towels before cutting it into bite-size pieces and adding it to the soy sauce mixture. Toss it through the marinade to coat, and set aside for 5 minutes.

Heat a wok until a drop of water evaporates in a second or two. Add the oil and onion and stir until fragrant and golden. Add the tofu and the marinade and stir-fry for 3 to 4 minutes. Add the tatsoi and toss until just wilted. Serve immediately.

Serves 4

daikon with ginger & soy sauce

see variations page 171

Daikon is a variety of large, white radish with a mild flavor; it varies greatly in size, from a few inches to over a foot long. It can be found in most Asian grocers, or try using jicama, turnip, or parsnip as a substitute. Serve this dish with rice or noodles.

3 tbsp. peanut or vegetable oil
2 oz. fresh ginger, finely chopped
2 cloves garlic, finely chopped
1 yellow onion, sliced
12 oz. daikon, thinly sliced

1 large red pepper, sliced
4 baby bok choy, quartered
2 tbsp. light soy sauce
2 tbsp. dark soy sauce

Heat a wok until a drop of water evaporates in a second or two. Add the oil, ginger, garlic, and onion and stir-fry until fragrant and golden. Add the daikon and stir-fry for 1 to 2 minutes before adding the red pepper. Stir-fry for 2 to 3 minutes, then add the bok choy and both soy sauces. Toss until the vegetables are crisp-tender and coated in sauce. Serve immediately.

Serves 4

mixed vegetables with hoisin sauce

see variations page 172

Hoisin is a commercially available Asian sauce that originated in China; it is used as a marinade and glaze for meat, as well as a sauce or dipping sauce. It is dark, thick, sweet, and salty, with a pungent flavor. Serve this dish with noodles.

2 tbsp. peanut or vegetable oil
1/2 oz. fresh ginger, finely chopped
2 cloves garlic, finely chopped
1 medium red onion, halved lengthwise, and chopped
2 carrots, thinly sliced
1 red bell pepper, cut into bite-size pieces

1 bunch of Chinese broccoli, cut into bite-size pieces
1 (8-oz.) can baby corn, drained and cut into bite-size pieces
1 (8-oz.) can sliced water chestnuts, drained
1/2 cup hoisin sauce
1 small bunch fresh cilantro, chopped

Heat a wok until a drop of water evaporates in a second or two. Add the oil, ginger, garlic, and onion, and stir-fry until fragrant and golden. Add the carrot and red pepper and stir-fry for 2 to 3 minutes.

Add the Chinese broccoli to the wok and toss for 1 to 2 minutes. Add the baby corn, water chestnuts, and hoisin sauce, tossing in the wok to coat all the ingredients with the sauce. Once the vegetables are crisp-tender, toss through half the cilantro and serve the stir-fry sprinkled with the remaining cilantro.

Serves 4

lotus root with ginger & scallions

see variations page 173

Fresh lotus root can be found at most Asian grocery stores. They should be a beige color when fresh; they tend to darken with age. Placing the prepared lotus root into a bowl of water with vinegar will prevent it from discoloring once cut. If fresh lotus root is unavailable, it can be purchased frozen or canned. Serve this dish with steamed greens and rice.

splash of vinegar
3–4 lotus roots
2 tbsp. peanut or vegetable oil
2 cloves garlic, finely chopped

1 bunch scallions, cut into bite-size pieces
1/4 cup light soy sauce
1/2 tsp. freshly ground black pepper

Fill a large bowl with cold water and a good splash of vinegar. Peel the lotus roots and cut into thin slices, placing each slice into the bowl of vinegar-water immediately. Just before cooking, drain the lotus roots well and pat dry with paper towels.

Heat a wok until a drop of water evaporates in a second or two. Add the oil, garlic, and scallions and stir-fry until fragrant and golden. Add the lotus roots and cook, tossing occasionally, for 3 to 4 minutes, until the lotus roots start to change color and look translucent. Add the soy sauce and pepper and stir-fry for 1 to 2 minutes more, until the lotus roots begin to look caramelized. Serve immediately.

Serves 4

broccoli & black bean

see base recipe page 123

peppers & black bean
Omit the broccoli and replace it with 2 red and 2 green bell peppers, cored and sliced, and complete the recipe as directed.

broccoli, tofu & black bean
Halve the broccoli. Add 12 ounces of very firm tofu, cut into bite-size pieces, to the wok after the garlic and onion, and stir-fry for 2 to 3 minutes before adding the broccoli. Complete the recipe as directed.

mixed vegetables in black bean sauce
Quarter the broccoli. After stir-frying the garlic and onion, add 1 peeled and sliced large carrot to the wok. Stir-fry for 30 seconds before adding 1 seeded and sliced large red bell pepper. Stir-fry for 1 to 2 minutes before adding the broccoli. Follow the remainder of the recipe, tossing 2 cups of baby spinach through the mixture with the first half of the cilantro.

broccoli & noodles in black bean sauce
Prepare 12 ounces of egg noodles according to package directions and add to the wok just after the cornstarch and water, and heat them through before serving. There is no need to serve this variation with rice.

variations

chile-eggplant

see base recipe page 124

chile-mushrooms
Replace the eggplant with 1 pound of sliced portobello mushrooms.

chili paste & eggplant
Omit the fresh chile and miso paste. Add 2 tablespoons of chili paste, such as sambal oelek or something milder, to the wok just after the eggplant. Complete the recipe as directed.

chile & basil eggplant
Add a small bunch chopped fresh basil to the eggplant just before serving.

chile-eggplant with peanuts
Add 1/2 cup of chopped, roasted peanuts to the eggplant just before serving.

variations

eggplant, tofu & tomato

see base recipe page 126

butternut squash, tofu & tomato
Substitute 1/2 a butternut squash, peeled, seeded and thinly sliced, for the eggplant.

eggplant, broccoli & tomato
Substitute 1 large head of broccoli cut into bite-size florets for the tofu.

bok choy, tofu & tomato
Omit the eggplant. Add the tofu to the stir-fry after the ginger, garlic, and onion. Add 6 baby bok choy, quartered, with the tomatoes.

eggplant, tofu & zucchini
Substitute 2 medium zucchini, sliced, for the tomatoes. Add a little vegetable broth or water if the stir-fry seems a little dry.

variations

ginger, tofu & asian greens

see base recipe page 128

spicy ginger & tofu
Add 1 tablespoon of sambal oelek to the wok with the ginger, garlic, and scallions.

garlic & chili tofu
Omit the ginger and increase the garlic to 4 cloves. Add 2 finely sliced long red chiles to the wok with the garlic and scallions.

ginger & tempeh
Substitute an equal amount of tempeh, cut into bite-size pieces, for the tofu.

ginger, tofu & mushroom
Omit the bok choy and cabbage. Add 1 pound of sliced button mushrooms to the wok just after the tofu, and stir-fry until softened before adding the sugar and soy sauce.

green vegetables with sesame

see base recipe page 129

rainbow vegetables with sesame
Prepare the basic recipe, but substitute 1 sliced large yellow onion for the broccoli;
2 sliced medium carrots for the green beans; and 1 sliced large red bell pepper for
the zucchini.

green vegetables with chile
Prepare the basic recipe, but omit the sesame seeds and sesame oil. Add 2 large red chiles,
seeded and finely sliced, to the wok with the garlic.

green vegetables with sesame & ginger
Add 1 1/2 ounces of fresh ginger, peeled and finely chopped, to the wok with the sesame
seeds and garlic and complete the recipe as directed.

green vegetables with cashews
Prepare the basic recipe, but omit the sesame seeds and sesame oil. Add 2/3 cup cashews to
the wok with the garlic. Garnish the dish with 1/2 cup toasted, chopped cashews.

variations

tempeh & green vegetables

see base recipe page 130

spicy tempeh & green vegetables
Prepare the basic recipe, but substitute hot chili sauce for the sweet chili sauce.

tempeh & red bell pepper
Prepare the basic recipe, but substitute 2 large red bell peppers, sliced into strips, for the green beans.

tempeh, green vegetables & sesame
Prepare the basic recipe, but add 1 tablespoon sesame oil and 2 tablespoons sesame seeds to the wok with the sweet chili and soy sauces. Garnish with extra sesame seeds.

tofu & green vegetables
Substitute 12 ounces of extra-firm tofu, cut into bite-size pieces, for the tempeh. Complete the recipe as directed.

variations

sweet chili & vegetables

see base recipe page 132

sweet chili & asian greens
Prepare the basic recipe, but omit the mushrooms and red bell pepper. Add the broccolini to the wok after the onion, with 1 bunch of Chinese flowering cabbage, roughly chopped. Stir-fry for 1 to 2 minutes then add 1/4 small Chinese cabbage, chopped, along with the baby spinach, water chestnuts, and sauces. Complete the recipe as directed.

hot chili & mixed vegetables
Prepare the basic recipe, but omit the sweet chili sauce. Use 2 long red chiles, seeded and finely sliced, and add 1/4 to 1/2 cup hot chili sauce, to taste, with the soy sauce.

sweet chili & basil vegetables
Prepare the basic recipe, but substitute a small bunch of chopped, fresh basil for the parsley.

sweet chili & cilantro vegetables
Prepare the basic recipe, but substitute a small bunch of chopped, fresh cilantro for the parsley.

variations

mixed mushrooms

see base recipe page 134

spicy mixed mushrooms
Prepare the basic recipe, but add 2 teaspoons of chili paste with the oyster and soy sauces.

green curry mushrooms
Prepare the basic recipe, but omit the oyster and soy sauces. Add 1 to 2 tablespoons of green curry paste to the wok with the garlic and scallions, and 1/2 cup coconut milk with the straw mushrooms.

mushroom & chinese cabbage
Add 1/4 small Chinese cabbage, shredded, to the wok with the straw mushrooms and sauces. Complete the recipe as directed.

mushroom & snow pea
Add 8 ounces of topped and tailed snow peas to the wok with the straw mushrooms and sauces. Complete the recipe as directed.

asian greens & oyster sauce

see base recipe page 135

asian greens & chili sauce
Prepare the basic recipe, but substitute 1/4 cup mild or hot chili sauce and 2 tablespoons soy sauce for the oyster sauce.

asian greens with basil & chile
Prepare the basic recipe, but omit the oyster sauce. Add two seeded, finely sliced red chiles to the wok with the ginger. Add 1/4 cup soy sauce and a small bunch of roughly chopped fresh basil to the wok with the Chinese cabbage.

broccoli & zucchini in oyster sauce
Omit the Chinese broccoli, bok choy, and Chinese cabbage. Add 1 large head of broccoli, cut into bite-size pieces, to the wok following the ginger. Stir-fry the broccoli for a few minutes before adding 2 sliced medium zucchini to the wok with the oyster sauce and tossing until the zucchini is tender.

asian greens with ginger & sesame
Prepare the basic recipe, but increase the ginger to 1 1/2 ounces and stir-fry as directed. Substitute 1 tablespoon sesame oil, 1/4 cup soy sauce, and 2 tablespoons sesame seeds for the oyster sauce. Garnish with extra sesame seeds.

variations

celery & red onion with black pepper & lime

see base recipe page 136

chinese broccoli & red onion with black pepper & lime
Substitute 1 1/2 pounds Chinese broccoli, cut into bite-size pieces, for the celery. Complete the recipe as directed.

celery & red onion with chili & lime
Prepare the basic recipe, but omit the black pepper. Add two finely sliced red chiles to the wok with the garlic and onions.

celery & red onion with Szechuan peppercorns & lime
Prepare the basic recipe, but omit the black pepper. Add 2 teaspoons of Szechuan peppercorns to the wok with the garlic and red onion.

celery & scallions with black pepper & lime
Prepare the basic recipe, but substitute 1 bunch of scallions, cut into bite-size pieces, for the red onion.

variations

seasoned lettuce

see base recipe page 138

seasoned cabbage
Prepare the basic recipe, but substitute 1 medium Chinese cabbage, torn into bite-size chunks, for the iceberg lettuce.

spicy lettuce
Add 1 to 2 teaspoons of chili paste to the soy sauce mixture. Complete the recipe as directed.

lettuce with ginger
Prepare the basic recipe, but increase the ginger to 1 1/2 ounces. If available, garnish the stir-fry with 2 tablespoons shredded pickled ginger.

lettuce with cilantro
Finely chop the bottoms of the stems of 1 small bunch of fresh cilantro and roughly chop the leaves. Add the stems to the wok with the ginger, garlic, and scallions. Add the leaves to the wok with the lettuce. Complete the recipe as directed.

tofu with green chili paste

see base recipe page 140

tofu with red chili paste
Substitute 3 long red chiles for the green chiles in the chili paste. Alternatively, replace the paste ingredients with 2 to 3 teaspoons (or more, if preferred) of prepared chili paste.

tofu with tamarind
Prepare the basic recipe, but reduce the green chiles to 1, and add 1 tablespoon tamarind paste to the paste mixture with the sesame oil. Stir-fry as before, adding 1/4 cup coconut milk to the wok with the soy sauce.

tofu with black bean
Prepare the basic recipe, but substitute 1 tablespoon fermented black beans for the green chiles in the paste and 2 teaspoons cornstarch mixed into 1/2 cup cold water for the soy sauce.

tempeh with green chili paste
Prepare the basic recipe, but substitute 12 ounces tempeh, cut into bite-size pieces, for the tofu.

garlic & pepper tofu

see base recipe page 142

garlic & pepper eggplant
Prepare the basic recipe, but substitute one large eggplant, halved and sliced, for the tofu.

chile & basil tofu
Halve the garlic and omit the black pepper. Add 2 finely sliced red chiles to the wok with the garlic and onion, and toss through 1 small bunch of chopped fresh basil just before serving.

garlic & chile tofu
Prepare the basic recipe, but omit the black pepper. Add 2 seeded and finely sliced red chiles to the wok with the garlic and onion.

szechuan peppercorns & tofu
Prepare the basic recipe, but omit the black pepper and halve the garlic. Add 2 teaspoons crushed Szechuan peppercorns to the wok with the garlic and onion.

variations

squash & peanuts

see base recipe page 144

zucchini & peanuts
Prepare the basic recipe, but substitute 2 sliced large zucchini for the butternut squash.

squash & cashews
Prepare the basic recipe, but substitute 1/4 cup light soy sauce and 2 teaspoons cornstarch for the peanut butter and 1/2 cup roasted cashews, chopped, for the roasted peanuts.

squash, bok choy & peanuts
Add 4 chopped baby bok choy to the wok just before the end of cooking, and allow them to wilt, but remain crisp, before adding the peanuts and cilantro.

squash, basil & garlic
Prepare the basic recipe, but omit the peanut butter, roasted peanuts, and cilantro. Add 1/4 cup light soy sauce and 2 teaspoons cornstarch to the sauce mixture, increase the garlic to 4 cloves, and replace the cilantro with 1 small bunch of fresh basil, chopped.

variations

cashews & mixed vegetables

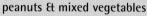

see base recipe page 146

peanuts & mixed vegetables
Prepare the basic recipe, but substitute 2/3 cup roasted and chopped peanuts for the cashews.

cashews, lime & mixed vegetables
Combine the zest and juice of one lime and 2 teaspoons sugar in a bowl, mix well, and add to the wok with the soy sauce. Complete the recipe as directed.

cashews, garlic & mixed vegetables
Prepare the basic recipe, but omit the green chile. Double the garlic, and garnish the finished stir-fry with 1 small bunch of finely chopped fresh garlic chives.

cashews & spicy vegetables
Prepare the basic recipe, but add 1 finely sliced red chile to the wok with the green chile, and add 1 to 2 teaspoons sambal oelek (see Glossary, page 280), to taste, with the soy sauce.

variations

marinated tofu

see base recipe page 148

marinated mushrooms
Prepare the basic recipe, but substitute 1 pound sliced mushrooms for the tofu.

spicy marinated tofu
Add 1 to 2 teaspoons sambal oelek to the marinade for the tofu. Garnish the stir-fry with sliced red chiles, if desired.

asian greens & marinated tofu
Prepare the basic recipe, but reduce the tatsoi to 4 ounces, and add 2 quartered baby bok choy and 1/8 of a Chinese cabbage, shredded, to the wok with the tatsoi.

marinated tofu with sesame
Prepare the basic recipe, but add 1 tablespoon sesame oil to the marinade and 1 tablespoon sesame seeds to the wok with the onion. Garnish the stir-fry with extra sesame seeds.

variations

daikon with ginger & soy sauce

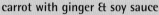

see base recipe page 150

carrot with ginger & soy sauce
Prepare the basic recipe, but substitute 3 sliced large carrots for the daikon.

daikon with chili & soy sauce
Reduce the ginger to 1 ounce. Add 2 finely sliced red chiles to the wok with the garlic and ginger. Complete the recipe as directed.

daikon with basil, chili & soy sauce
Reduce the ginger to 1 ounce. Add 2 finely sliced red chiles to the wok with the garlic and ginger, and 1/2 small bunch of chopped fresh basil at the end of cooking. Garnish with additional basil.

daikon with garlic & soy sauce
Reduce the ginger to 1/2 ounce, and increase the garlic to 4 cloves, finely chopped. Garnish with a few finely chopped garlic chives.

variations

mixed vegetables with hoisin sauce

see base recipe page 152

asian greens with hoisin sauce
Omit the carrot, red bell pepper, and baby corn. Add 1 bunch Chinese flowering cauliflower, chopped, to the wok after the onions, and stir-fry until just tender before adding the Chinese broccoli. Stir-fry for 1 to 2 minutes more before adding 1/4 of a small Chinese cabbage, chopped, to the wok with the water chestnuts and hoisin sauce.

mixed vegetables with oyster sauce
Prepare the basic recipe, but substitute 1/2 cup of oyster sauce for the hoisin sauce.

vegetable & tofu with hoisin sauce
Omit the baby corn and water chestnuts. Rinse, drain, and pat dry 12 ounces extra-firm tofu and cut into bite-size pieces. Add to the wok after the ginger, garlic, and onion, and stir-fry for 2 to 3 minutes before adding the carrot and pepper.

mushrooms with hoisin sauce
Substitute 1 pound sliced mixed mushrooms (shitake, button, oyster, and portobello) for the carrot and red bell pepper, and stir-fry until they color and soften.

lotus root with ginger & scallions

see base recipe page 154

lotus root with ginger & lemon
Combine the zest and juice of one lemon and 2 teaspoons sugar in a bowl, and mix well. Peel and finely chop 1 1/2 ounces fresh ginger. Add the ginger to the wok with the garlic and scallions, and the lemon mixture with the soy sauce and pepper. Complete the recipe as directed.

lotus root with sesame & scallions
Add 2 tablespoons sesame seeds to the wok with the garlic and scallions. Add 1 tablespoon sesame oil with the soy sauce. Garnish with extra sesame seeds.

lotus root with chile & scallions
Prepare the basic recipe, but add 2 finely sliced red chiles to the wok with the garlic and scallions.

lotus root with peanuts, ginger & chile
Finely chop 1 1/2 ounces fresh ginger, finely slice 2 red chiles, and roughly chop 2/3 cup roasted peanuts. Add the ginger and chiles to the wok with the garlic and scallions. Toss the peanuts through the finished stir-fry just before serving.

fish & seafood

Fish and seafood have always been an important part of Asian culture, with many specific types used in traditional and ceremonial dishes. Fish and seafood are well suited to stir-frying, because most cook quickly. Plus they readily take on accompanying flavors, particularly as many Asian sauces and flavorings are fish or seafood based.

salmon with lemongrass

see variations page 208

Salmon works extremely well in stir-fry dishes; it's strong enough to not get lost in other intense flavors, and its firm flesh means that it doesn't fall apart easily. Take extra care to remove all small pin-bones. These can be felt by running your finger along the fish, and removed by pulling them out with a pair of tweezers. Serve this dish with rice.

1/4 cup light soy sauce
1 tbsp. sesame oil
1 tbsp. lemon juice
2 tsp. coconut palm sugar or brown sugar
1 stalk lemongrass, outer leaves and root
    discarded, white part finely chopped
2 cloves garlic, finely chopped

1/2 oz. fresh ginger, finely chopped
1 lb. skinless salmon, pin-boned and cut into
    bite-size pieces
2 tbsp. peanut or vegetable oil
4 scallions, cut into bite-size pieces
1/4 small Chinese cabbage, torn into
    bite-size pieces

Combine the soy sauce, sesame oil, lemon juice, sugar, lemongrass, garlic, and ginger in a bowl and add the salmon pieces, tossing gently to coat. Let marinate for 10 minutes.

Heat a wok until a drop of water evaporates in a second or two. Add the peanut or vegetable oil and scallions and stir-fry until just golden. Add the salmon, reserving the marinade. Stir-fry the salmon for 2 to 3 minutes, until just cooked, then add the Chinese cabbage and reserved marinade, stir-frying until just wilted but still crisp. Serve immediately.

Serves 4

calamari with bok choy & shitake mushroom

see variations page 209

Calamari tubes – slices of the body – can be purchased fresh and cleaned. To prepare whole calamari, pull the tentacles away from the body. Cut off the tentacles and discard the head, innards, and wings. Remove the skin from the body by running your fingers under it and peeling it off. Remove the backbone and rinse the tube. Prepare the tube as required, and slice the tentacles into lengths. Serve this dish with rice.

1 lb. calamari tubes
2 tbsp. peanut or vegetable oil
2 cloves garlic, finely chopped
1 oz. fresh ginger, finely chopped
1/2 lb. fresh shitake mushrooms, sliced

6 baby bok choy, quartered lengthwise
2 tbsp. light soy sauce
3 tbsp. oyster sauce
1 tsp. cornstarch
1/4 cup cold water

Cut the calamari tubes in half lengthwise, score the insides diagonally in a diamond pattern, and slice them into strips. Heat a wok until a drop of water evaporates in a second or two. Add the oil, garlic, and ginger and stir-fry until fragrant and golden. Add the mushrooms and toss for 1 to 2 minutes, until they start to soften and color. Add the calamari to the wok and stir-fry until it just begins to turn opaque. Add the bok choy and toss for 1 minute, until it begins to wilt. Add the soy sauce and oyster sauce, tossing to combine. Mix the cornstarch and water, add it to the wok and stir immediately to prevent lumps from forming. Cook for about 1 minute, until the sauce is thick and bubbling and everything is coated.

Serves 4

salmon & ginger soba noodles with sesame

see variations page 210

Japanese soba noodles are made from buckwheat flour. They are gray-brown and have an earthy flavor with a firm texture. They can be found in most grocery stores, and can be substituted for ramen or udon noodles. Just cook according to the package directions.

10 oz. dry soba noodles
1/4 cup light soy sauce
1 tbsp. sesame oil
2 cloves garlic, finely chopped
1 1/2 oz. fresh ginger, finely chopped
1 lb. skinless salmon, pin-boned and cut into
    bite-size pieces

2 tbsp. peanut or vegetable oil
4 scallions, cut into bite-size pieces
2 tbsp. sesame seeds
8 oz. snow peas, topped and tailed
2 tbsp. rice wine
2 tsp. cornstarch
1/2 cup cold water

Cook the noodles according to the package directions and set aside. Combine the soy sauce, sesame oil, garlic, and ginger in a bowl and add the salmon. Let marinate for 10 minutes.

Heat a wok until a drop of water evaporates in a second or two. Add the peanut or vegetable oil, scallions, and sesame seeds and stir-fry until fragrant and golden. Add the salmon and marinade and stir-fry for 2 to 3 minutes, until nearly cooked. Add the snow peas, noodles, and rice wine and toss until the snow peas are tender. Mix the cornstarch and water, add it to the wok and stir immediately to prevent lumps from forming. Cook the sauce for about 1 minute, until it is thick and bubbling. Serve immediately.

Serves 4

octopus & eggplant

see variations page 211

Baby octopus can be found at most large grocery stores, cleaned and ready to use. If whole, they can easily be cleaned by cutting a slit at the base of the head, removing the innards and then cutting away the hard beak. Rinse under cold, running water before using. Alternatively, substitute with an equal amount of shrimp or calamari.

3 tbsp. peanut or vegetable oil, divided
1 lb. cleaned and de-beaked baby octopus
2 long red chiles, seeded and finely sliced
2 cloves garlic, finely chopped
4 scallions, sliced
2 medium eggplant, halved and sliced into strips
2 tbsp. kecap manis
3 tbsp. light soy sauce
2 tbsp. sweet chili sauce
1 tbsp. sesame oil
1/4 cup water
1 small bunch fresh Thai basil, chopped
chopped scallions, if desired

Heat a wok until a drop of water evaporates in a second or two. Add 1 tablespoon of the peanut or vegetable oil and the octopus and stir-fry the octopus for 2 to 3 minutes, until just cooked. Remove the octopus to a plate, cover, and set aside.

Add the remaining peanut or vegetable oil to the wok; heat until smoking and then add the chile, garlic, and scallions and stir-fry until fragrant and golden. Add the eggplant and toss for 2 to 3 minutes, until the eggplant is golden and starting to soften. Stir in the kecap manis, soy sauce, sweet chili sauce, sesame oil, and water and stir-fry for 2 to 3 minutes, until the eggplant has softened and absorbed the juices. Return the octopus and any juices to the wok and toss to combine. Once the octopus has heated through, toss through half the Thai basil. Sprinkle with the remaining basil and chopped scallions, if desired.

Serves 4

chile & thai basil shellfish

see variations page 212

Before using fresh shellfish, pick over and remove any with broken or open shells that don't close up after tapping them on a work surface, because they are dead and not good to use. Shellfish should smell like fresh seawater and the shells should be closed tight. Serve this dish with rice or noodles.

2 tbsp. peanut or vegetable oil
1 oz. fresh ginger, finely chopped
2 cloves garlic, finely chopped
2–3 long red chiles, seeded and finely sliced
6 scallions
2 lb. shellfish (mussels, clams) soaked and
   scrubbed in cold water to remove grit
   and seaweed

2 large tomatoes, chopped
1/4 cup light soy sauce
2 tbsp. rice wine
1 tbsp. sweet chili sauce
2 tsp. chili sauce
1 small bunch fresh Thai basil, chopped

Heat a wok until a drop of water evaporates in a second or two. Add the oil, ginger, garlic, chiles, and scallions and stir-fry until fragrant and beginning to color. Add the shellfish and tomatoes, tossing for 1 to 2 minutes.

Add the soy sauce, rice wine, sweet chili sauce, and chili sauce and stir quickly to combine, then put a lid on the wok. Steam for 3 to 4 minutes, until the shellfish have cooked and most of the shells have opened — discard any that don't. Use a slotted spoon to remove the shellfish from the wok to a serving dish, then add the chopped Thai basil to the sauce in the wok. Simmer for 1 minute, season to taste, then spoon over the shellfish. Serve immediately.

Serves 4

korean-style fish

see variations page 213

Any firm, white fish can be used in this recipe; more delicate, flakier fish tends to break up and fall apart when being stir-fried. Suitable fish include halibut, cod, orange roughy, or sea bass. Serve this dish with rice or noodles.

1/4 cup light soy sauce
1 tbsp. sesame oil
1 tbsp. rice wine
2 cloves garlic, finely chopped
1 tsp. chili powder
2 tbsp. sesame seeds

1 lb. firm, skinless white fish, de-boned and cut
    into bite-size pieces
2 tbsp. peanut or vegetable oil
4 scallions, cut into bite-size pieces
1 large red bell pepper, cut into bite-size pieces
8 baby bok choy, cut into bite-size pieces
1/4 cup water, if needed

Combine the soy sauce, sesame oil, rice wine, garlic, chili powder, and sesame seeds in a bowl and add the fish, tossing gently to coat. Let marinate for 10 minutes.

Heat a wok until a drop of water evaporates in a second or two. Add the peanut or vegetable oil, followed by the scallions, and stir-fry until fragrant and golden before adding the bell peppers. Stir-fry until the peppers are tender then add the fish and marinade to the wok and stir-fry for 2 to 3 minutes, until nearly cooked.

Add the bok choy and water, if needed, and cook for 1 to 2 minutes, until the bok choy has wilted. Serve immediately.

Serves 4

honey, ginger & lime shrimp

see variations page 214

Prepare whole shrimp by removing the head from the body and peeling away the shell in segments. The tail can be left on if desired. Once peeled, slice along the back of the shrimp and use the tip of the knife to remove the vein that runs through it. Alternatively, use peeled and deveined shrimp as directed. Serve with noodles or rice.

2 tbsp. peanut or vegetable oil
1 medium yellow onion, halved lengthwise
    and chopped
1 1/2 oz. fresh ginger, finely chopped
1 lb. peeled and deveined large shrimp

1 bunch Chinese broccoli, cut into
    bite-size pieces
8 baby bok choy, cut into bite-size pieces
2 tbsp. honey
zest and juice of 1 lime
2 tbsp. fish sauce

Heat a wok until a drop of water evaporates in a second or two. Add the oil, onion, and ginger and stir-fry until fragrant and beginning to color. Add the shrimp and toss for 2 to 3 minutes until the shrimp are just turning opaque.

Add the Chinese broccoli and cook for 1 to 2 minutes, until just tender. Add the bok choy, honey, lime zest and juice, and fish sauce and stir-fry until the bok choy has wilted. Serve immediately.

Serves 4

pork & shrimp

see variations page 215

Pork and shrimp complement each other beautifully in this dish. Rice vermicelli is angel hair rice noodles, sold dry. They can usually be found in the noodle section of the grocery store, but can be substituted for any dry rice noodle, cooked to package directions.

8 oz. dry rice vermicelli	2 tbsp. peanut or vegetable oil	2 medium carrots, sliced
1/2 cup chicken broth	8 oz. pork fillet, sliced	10 oz. peeled and deveined
2 tbsp. light soy sauce	1 tsp. curry powder	shrimp
1 tbsp. rice wine	1 medium red onion, halved	8 oz. mung bean sprouts
1 tbsp. coconut palm sugar	lengthwise, and sliced	4 scallions, chopped
or brown sugar	2 cloves garlic, finely chopped	

Put the rice vermicelli into a heatproof bowl and cover with boiling water; let sit for 1 to 2 minutes, until softened, then drain. Set aside. Combine the chicken broth, soy sauce, rice wine, and sugar in a bowl and set aside.

Heat a wok until a drop of water evaporates in a second or two. Add half of the oil and the pork fillet and stir-fry until browned and just cooked. Remove to a plate, cover, and set aside.

Add the remaining oil to the wok, heat until just smoking, and add the curry powder, red onion, and garlic and stir-fry until fragrant and beginning to color. Add the carrots and stir-fry for 1 to 2 minutes, then add the shrimp, tossing for 2 to 3 minutes, until turning opaque. Return the pork to the wok, then add the noodles, broth mixture, and bean sprouts. Toss for 2 to 3 minutes, until everything is combined and hot. Serve sprinkled with the scallions.

Serves 4

szechuan peppercorn tuna

see variations page 216

Fresh tuna works well in stir-fries, because it has a firm texture and good flavor.
Choose only the freshest fish. Salmon makes an acceptable substitute if you cannot
find fresh tuna. Serve this dish with rice.

1/4 cup light soy sauce
1 tbsp. sesame oil
1 tbsp. chili sauce
2 tsp. coconut palm sugar
   or brown sugar
2 cloves garlic, finely chopped

1 lb. skinless tuna, cut into
   bite-size pieces
3 tbsp. peanut or vegetable
   oil
2 tsp. Szechuan peppercorns
2 fresh red chiles, chopped

4 scallions, cut into bite-size
   pieces
1 lb. stringless green beans,
   topped and tailed and cut
   into bite-size pieces

Combine the soy sauce, sesame oil, chili sauce, sugar, and garlic in a bowl and add the tuna,
tossing gently to coat. Let sit for 10 minutes.

Heat a wok until a drop of water evaporates in a second or two. Add the peanut or vegetable
oil, Szechuan peppercorns, and chiles and stir-fry for 10 seconds before adding the scallions
and beans. Stir-fry for a few minutes, until the beans start to blister and crinkle. Add the
tuna and marinade and stir-fry for 3 to 4 minutes, until just cooked. Serve immediately.

Serves 4

fish & vegetables

see variations page 217

Most vegetables are suitable for stir-frying; just add them to the wok in order of firmness. Firmer vegetables such as peppers, celery, and root vegetables take the longest to cook. Serve this dish with noodles or rice.

2 tbsp. light soy sauce
1 tbsp. fish sauce
1 tsp. coconut palm sugar or brown sugar
2 tbsp. peanut or vegetable oil
1 lb. firm, skinless white fish, de-boned and cut into bite-size pieces
1 medium yellow onion, halved lengthwise, and sliced

2 cloves garlic, finely chopped
1 large carrot, sliced
1 large red bell pepper, cut into bite-size pieces
1 bunch of broccolini, cut into bite-size pieces
3 oz. baby spinach
1 (8-oz.) can sliced water chestnuts, drained
1 small bunch fresh cilantro, chopped

Combine the light soy sauce, fish sauce, and sugar in a bowl and stir to dissolve the sugar. Set aside.

Heat a wok until a drop of water evaporates in a second or two. Add half of the oil and the fish and stir-fry the fish for 2 to 3 minutes until just cooked. Remove the fish to a plate, cover, and set aside.

Add the remainder of the oil, the garlic, and onion to the wok and stir-fry until fragrant and golden. Add the carrot and bell pepper and toss until the carrot and pepper are tender. Add the broccolini and fry for 1 minute.

Return the fish and any juices to the wok. Immediately add the spinach, water chestnuts, and soy mixture. Cook for 1 minute, until the spinach has wilted, then toss through half the cilantro. Sprinkle with the remaining cilantro and serve immediately.

Serves 4

calamari with asian greens

see variations page 218

Fresh Asian greens can be found in Asian food stores and some grocery stores. Many of them have several names, but any variety of leafy greens can be used in this recipe. Add those with thick stems to the wok first, and leafy greens last. Serve with rice or noodles.

1 lb. calamari tubes
2 tbsp. peanut or vegetable oil
2 cloves garlic, finely chopped
6 scallions, cut into bite-size pieces
1 bunch Chinese flowering cabbage, cut into
    bite-size pieces

1 small bunch garlic chives, chopped
2 tbsp. light soy sauce
1 tbsp. dark soy sauce
1 tbsp. sweet chili sauce
1 small bunch fresh cilantro, chopped

Cut the calamari tubes in half lengthwise, score the insides diagonally in a diamond pattern, then slice them into strips. Heat a wok until a drop of water evaporates in a second or two. Add half of the oil and the calamari to the wok. Stir-fry the calamari for 2 to 3 minutes until just cooked, then remove to a plate, cover, and set aside.

Add the remainder of the oil to the wok; allow it to heat to smoking and then add the garlic and scallions and stir-fry until fragrant and golden. Add the Chinese flowering cabbage and stir-fry until just tender.

Add the garlic chives and the calamari and any juices to the wok. Add both soy sauces and the sweet chili sauce and toss to combine. Toss through half the cilantro. Sprinkle with the remaining cilantro and serve immediately.

Serves 4

lemon-pepper calamari

see variations page 219

Lemon and pepper is a classic combination that lends itself nicely to stir-fries. The acid in the lemon juice will slightly tenderize the calamari before cooking. Lime juice could be substituted for lemon. Serve this dish with rice.

zest and juice of 1 lemon
2 tbsp. light soy sauce
2 tsp. fish sauce
1 tbsp. coconut palm sugar or brown sugar
1 lb. calamari tubes
2 tbsp. peanut or vegetable oil
1 tsp. crushed black peppercorns

2 cloves garlic, finely chopped
1 red onion, halved lengthwise, and chopped
1 large red bell pepper, cut into bite-size pieces
1 bunch Chinese broccoli, cut into bite-size pieces
6 baby bok choy, quartered

Combine the lemon zest and juice, light soy sauce, fish sauce, and sugar in a bowl. Cut the calamari tubes in half lengthwise, score the insides diagonally in a diamond pattern, and slice them into strips.

Heat a wok until a drop of water evaporates in a second or two. Add the oil and crushed peppercorns and stir-fry for 10 seconds before adding the garlic and red onion. Stir-fry until fragrant and golden and then add the bell pepper and toss until just tender.

Add the calamari to the wok and toss for 2 to 3 minutes, until the calamari is just opaque. Add the lemon mixture and Chinese broccoli and stir-fry for 1 to 2 minutes. Add the bok choy and cook until it is wilted and the calamari is cooked through. Serve immediately.

Serves 4

shrimp paste & fish

see variations page 220

Shrimp paste has a pungent smell that can be overwhelming, but the flavor is not quite as strong once cooked. This recipe uses a small amount as a seasoning. Serve with rice.

2 tbsp. fish sauce
2 tsp. coconut palm sugar or brown sugar
1 lb. firm, skinless white fish, such as cod, sea bass, halibut, or orange roughy, de-boned and cut into bite-size pieces
2 tbsp. peanut or vegetable oil, divided
1 medium red onion, halved lengthwise, and chopped

2 cloves garlic, finely chopped
2 tsp. shrimp paste
1/4 cup water
1/8 of a small Chinese cabbage, cut into bite-size pieces
1 (8-oz.) can water chestnuts, drained
1 (8-oz.) can baby corn, drained
8 oz. mung bean sprouts

Combine the fish sauce and sugar in a bowl and stir to dissolve the sugar, add the fish and toss to coat. Set aside.

Heat a wok until a drop of water evaporates in a second or two. Add half of the oil and the fish to the wok and stir-fry for 2 to 3 minutes, until the fish is just cooked. Remove the fish to a plate, cover, and set aside. Add the remainder of the oil, onion, and garlic to the wok and stir-fry until fragrant and golden. Add the shrimp paste and water and stir-fry for a few seconds. Add the cabbage, water chestnuts, and baby corn and toss for 1 to 2 minutes, until the cabbage begins to wilt. Return the fish and any juices to the wok, then add the bean sprouts. Cook for 1 minute, until the fish is hot and the bean sprouts are just tender. Serve immediately.

Serves 4

singapore chili shrimp

see variations page 221

Based on a traditional Singaporean dish, these chili shrimp have beaten eggs stirred through. The egg will cook almost as soon as it is added to the hot sauce, so it is only added near the end of cooking. Serve this dish with rice and extra chili sauce if desired.

1 cup chicken broth
1/2 cup ketchup
1 tbsp. white vinegar
2 tsp. chili sauce
2 tsp. salt
2 tbsp. peanut or vegetable oil
2 long red chiles, seeded and finely chopped
1 oz. fresh ginger, finely chopped

3 cloves garlic, finely chopped
6 scallions, chopped
1 1/2 lb. peeled and deveined shrimp
4 baby bok choy, chopped
1 tbsp. cornstarch,
1/4 cup cold water
1 egg, beaten

Put the chicken broth, ketchup, vinegar, chili sauce, and salt into a small saucepan over medium heat. Bring to a boil, then reduce the heat to very low to keep the sauce hot.

Heat a wok until a drop of water evaporates in a second or two. Add the oil, chiles, ginger, garlic, and scallions and stir-fry until fragrant and beginning to color. Add the shrimp, tossing for 1 to 2 minutes, until the shrimp are just turning opaque.

Reduce the heat slightly and add the hot sauce and bok choy to the wok. Allow it to simmer while mixing the cornstarch and water and adding it to the wok. Stir immediately to prevent lumps from forming and cook the sauce for about 1 minute, until it is thick and bubbling. Stir in the beaten egg and serve immediately.

Serves 4

shrimp with lemon & peas

see variations page 222

Shrimp marry well with lemon and peas. Try serving this dish with rice that has been steamed with some bruised lemongrass for an extra lemony flavor or alternatively, with noodles.

2 tbsp. peanut or vegetable oil
1 medium red onion, chopped
2 cloves garlic, finely chopped
1 lb. peeled and deveined shrimp
2 cups frozen garden peas, defrosted

1/2 lb. snow peas, sliced
zest and juice of 1 lemon
2 tbsp. fish sauce
1 tbsp. light soy sauce
1 tsp. coconut palm sugar or brown sugar

Heat a wok until a drop of water evaporates in a second or two. Add the oil, red onion, and garlic and stir-fry until fragrant and beginning to color. Add the shrimp, tossing for 2 to 3 minutes, until the shrimp are just turning opaque.

Add the garden peas and cook for 1 minute more, until just tender, and then add the snow peas, lemon zest and juice, fish sauce, soy sauce, and sugar. Stir-fry until the vegetables are just tender. Serve immediately.

Serves 4

thai coconut fish

see variations page 223

Coconut milk adds a mild sweetness to stir-fries and is readily available in cans. Choose one that only contains coconut and water. Serve this dish with rice

1/2 cup plus 2 tbsp. coconut milk
2 tbsp. fish sauce
2 Kaffir lime leaves, shredded
1 tbsp. sweet chili sauce
1 tsp. coconut palm sugar or brown sugar
2 cloves garlic, finely chopped
1 lb. skinless, firm white fish, such as sea bass,
    cod, halibut or orange roughy, de-boned and
    cut into bite-size pieces
2 tbsp. peanut or vegetable oil

1 stalk lemongrass, outer leaves and root
    discarded, white part finely chopped
1 long red chile, seeded and finely sliced
6 scallions, cut into bite-size pieces
8 oz. snow peas, topped and tailed
4 oz. mung bean sprouts
1 (8-oz.) can sliced water chestnuts, drained
1/2 small bunch fresh cilantro, chopped
red chile, sliced

Combine the 2 tablespoons coconut milk, fish sauce, lime leaves, sweet chili sauce, sugar, and garlic in a bowl and add the fish, tossing gently to coat. Let marinate for 10 minutes.

Heat a wok until a drop of water evaporates in a second or two. Add the oil, lemongrass, red chile, and scallions and stir-fry until fragrant and golden. Add the fish and marinade and stir-fry for 2 to 3 minutes, until just opaque. Add the snow peas, bean sprouts, water chestnuts, and 1/2 cup coconut milk to the wok, bring to a simmer and cook, stirring, until the vegetables are crisp-tender and the fish is cooked through. Garnish with fresh cilantro and sliced red chile. Serve immediately.

Serves 4

tamarind & chile shrimp

see variations page 224

Tamarind is the sticky pulp from the pods of the tamarind tree. It can be found in a ready-to-use paste form in the Asian section of grocery stores. It has a distinctive sweet and sour taste, but, if unavailable, can be replaced with equal parts brown sugar and lime juice. Serve this dish with rice or noodles.

2 tbsp. peanut or vegetable oil
1 medium red onion, halved lengthwise, and sliced
2 long red chiles, seeded and finely sliced
2 cloves garlic, finely chopped
1 lb. peeled and deveined shrimp

1 tbsp. tamarind paste
1 tbsp. coconut palm sugar or brown sugar
2 tbsp. light soy sauce
2 large tomatoes, chopped
8 oz. snow peas, sliced
4 oz. baby spinach

Heat a wok until a drop of water evaporates in a second or two. Add the oil, red onion, red chiles, and garlic and stir-fry until fragrant and beginning to color. Add the shrimp, tossing for 1 to 2 minutes, until the shrimp are just starting to change color.

Add the tamarind paste, sugar, light soy sauce, and tomatoes and stir-fry for 1 to 2 minutes, until the tomatoes are starting to soften. Add the snow peas and stir-fry until tender. Add the baby spinach and toss until well combined and wilted. Serve immediately.

Serves 4

sweet chili mussels with lotus root

see variations page 225

Use a scourer to scrub any debris from the mussels and discard any with cracked shells.
Tap mussels with open shells on the counter top, and if they don't close, discard them.
The hairy beard that pokes out between the mussel shells can be removed by pinching it
and pulling from side to side until it comes away. Serve this dish with rice or noodles.

splash of vinegar
1 large lotus root
2 tbsp. peanut or vegetable oil
1 oz. fresh ginger, finely chopped
2 cloves garlic, finely chopped
1 long red chile seeded and finely sliced
6 scallions, chopped

2 lb. mussels, soaked and scrubbed in cold
    water to remove grit and seaweed
1/4 cup water
2 tbsp. light soy sauce
1/2 cup sweet chili sauce
1 tsp. chili sauce
1 small bunch fresh cilantro, chopped, plus
    extra for the garnish

Fill a large bowl with cold water and a splash of vinegar. Peel the lotus root and cut it
into thin slices, putting each slice into the bowl of vinegar water immediately. Just before
cooking, drain the lotus root well and pat dry on paper towels.

Heat a wok until a drop of water evaporates in a second or two. Add the oil, ginger, garlic,
chile, and scallions and stir-fry until fragrant and beginning to color. Add the lotus root,
tossing for 3 to 4 minutes, until it begins to look translucent.

Add the mussels, water, and soy sauce and toss to combine before placing a lid on the wok.
Steam for 3 to 4 minutes, until the mussels have cooked and most of the shells have opened
— discard any that don't open.

Use a slotted spoon to remove the mussels and lotus root from the wok to a serving dish. Add the sweet chili and chili sauces to the wok, simmer for a minute, stir in the cilantro, then spoon the sauce onto the dish and garnish with cilantro, if desired. Serve immediately.

Serves 4

calamari, black bean & cucumber

see variations page 226

Although they are usually used in salads, cucumbers shine in stir-fry dishes and their mild flavor and crunch make them an addition worth considering. Add them toward the end of cooking so they retain their crunch. Serve this dish with rice.

1 lb. calamari tubes
2 tbsp. peanut or vegetable oil
2 cloves garlic, peeled and finely chopped
1 oz. fresh ginger, finely sliced

1 red onion, halved lengthwise, and sliced
2/3 cup black bean sauce
2 large cucumbers, halved, seeded, and sliced

Cut the calamari tubes in half lengthwise, score the insides diagonally in a diamond pattern, and slice them into strips. Set aside.

Heat a wok until a drop of water evaporates in a second or two. Add the oil, garlic, ginger, and red onion and stir-fry until fragrant and golden. Add the calamari and toss for 1 to 2 minutes, until just opaque.

Add the black bean sauce and cucumber and stir-fry until the calamari is cooked and the cucumber hot. Serve immediately.

Serves 4

ginger fish

see variations page 227

The mushrooms in this recipe help to give the dish an earthy flavor. Try using one or two of the many mushrooms and fungi that can be found fresh and dried in many Asian grocery stores. Serve this dish with rice.

1/4 cup light soy sauce
1 tbsp. fish sauce
1 tsp. coconut palm sugar or brown sugar
2 tbsp. peanut or vegetable oil, divided
1 lb. firm, skinless white fish, such as cod, halibut, orange roughy, or sea bass, de-boned and cut into bite-size pieces
1 1/2 oz. fresh ginger, cut into matchsticks

2 cloves garlic, finely chopped
1 medium yellow onion, halved lengthwise, and chopped
6 small to medium portobello mushrooms, sliced
1 large red bell pepper, cut into bite-size pieces
1 large head of broccoli, cut into bite-size florets
4 scallions, chopped

Combine the light soy sauce, fish sauce, and sugar in a bowl and stir to dissolve the sugar. Set aside.

Heat a wok until a drop of water evaporates in a second or two. Add half the oil and the fish and stir-fry for 2 to 3 minutes until the fish is just cooked. Remove the fish from the wok to a plate, cover, and set aside.

Add the remainder of the oil, ginger, garlic, and onion to the wok and stir-fry until fragrant and golden. Add the mushrooms and bell pepper and toss until they start to soften and color. Add the broccoli and stir for a minute more.

Return the fish and any juices to the wok, then add the soy sauce mixture. Cook for
1 minute, until the vegetables are crisp-tender, then toss through half the scallions. Sprinkle
with the remaining scallions and serve immediately.

Serves 4

variations

salmon with lemongrass

see base recipe page 175

shrimp with lemongrass
Prepare the basic recipe, but substitute 1 pound peeled and deveined shrimp for the salmon.

salmon with chili & lemongrass
Prepare the basic recipe, adding 2 long red chiles, seeded and finely sliced, to the wok with the scallions. Complete the recipe as directed.

fish with cilantro & lemongrass
Prepare the basic recipe, but substitute 1 pound of skinless white fish, bones removed and fish cut into bite-size pieces, for the salmon. Add the finely chopped roots of 1 small bunch fresh cilantro to the soy sauce mixture. Complete the recipe as directed and garnish the stir-fry with chopped fresh cilantro.

salmon with ginger & lemongrass
Increase the ginger to 1 1/2 ounces and complete the recipe as directed.

variations

calamari with bok choy & shitake mushroom

see base recipe page 176

shrimp, bok choy & shitake mushroom
Prepare the basic recipe, but omit the calamari. Add 1 pound peeled and deveined shrimp to the wok after the mushrooms and stir-fry until just opaque before adding the bok choy and remaining ingredients.

calamari, spinach & shitake mushroom
Prepare the basic recipe, but omit the bok choy. Add 8 ounces baby spinach to the wok with the soy sauce and oyster sauce.

calamari, bok choy & noodles
Prepare the basic recipe, but omit the shitake mushrooms. Prepare 12 ounces fresh udon noodles according to package directions, and add to the wok with the bok choy. There is no need to serve this variation with rice.

calamari, bok choy & button mushroom
Prepare the basic recipe, but substitute 8 ounces sliced button mushrooms for the shitake mushrooms.

variations

salmon & ginger soba noodles with sesame

see base recipe page 178

tuna & ginger soba noodles with sesame
Prepare the basic recipe, but substitute 1 pound of fresh skinless tuna, cut into bite-size pieces, for the salmon.

salmon & ginger soba noodles with lime
Prepare the basic recipe, but substitute the zest and juice of 1 lime and 1 teaspoon of sugar for the rice wine.

shrimp & ginger soba noodles with sesame
Prepare the basic recipe, but substitute 1 pound peeled and deveined shrimp for the salmon.

salmon & ginger rice noodles with sesame
Omit the soba noodles. Prepare 10 ounces dry rice noodles following the package directions, and add to the stir-fry in place of the soba noodles.

octopus & eggplant

see base recipe page 180

shrimp & eggplant
Prepare the basic recipe, but substitute 1 pound peeled and deveined shrimp for the octopus.

octopus & bell pepper
Prepare the basic recipe, but substitute 3 red bell peppers, cut into bite-size pieces, for the eggplant.

octopus & eggplant with basil
Prepare the basic recipe, but substitute 1 small bunch of roughly chopped fresh sweet basil for the Thai basil.

octopus, green vegetable & chili
Omit the eggplant. Prepare the basic recipe, replacing the eggplant with 1 large green bell pepper, cut into bite-size pieces, and 1 large head of broccoli, cut into bite-size florets. Add 4 ounces baby spinach to the stir-fry when returning the octopus to the wok.

variations

chile & thai basil shellfish

see base recipe page 181

chile & cilantro shellfish
Omit the Thai basil. Finely chop the roots of 1 small bunch of cilantro and roughly chop the leaves. Prepare the recipe as directed, adding the finely chopped roots to the wok with the ginger, garlic, and chili. Complete the recipe, replacing the Thai basil with the chopped cilantro leaves.

chile, basil & garlic shellfish
Omit the Thai basil from the basic recipe. Prepare the recipe as before, increasing the garlic to 4 cloves, peeled and finely chopped. Continue the recipe as instructed, replacing the Thai basil with 1 small bunch of chopped sweet basil.

chile & thai basil shrimp
Prepare the basic recipe, but omit the shellfish. Replace the shellfish with 2 pounds whole peeled and deveined shrimp.

ginger & thai basil shellfish
Prepare the basic recipe, increasing the ginger to 1 1/2 ounces, finely chopped. For a more decorative finish to the stir-fry, cut the ginger into fine matchsticks.

variations

korean-style fish

see base recipe page 182

vietnamese-style fish
Omit the marinade. Combine 1 tablespoon sugar, 2 tablespoons fish sauce, 2 teaspoons lemon juice, and the finely chopped lower stems of 1 small bunch fresh cilantro. Use this to marinate the fish, then complete the recipe as directed. Garnish with cilantro leaves.

korean-style shrimp
Prepare the basic recipe, but substitute 1 pound peeled and deveined shrimp for the white fish.

malaysian-style fish
Omit the marinade from the basic recipe. Combine 2 tablespoons kecap manis, the zest and juice of 1 lime, 1 tablespoon sugar, and 1 long red chile, seeded and finely sliced. Use this mixture to marinate the fish, then complete the recipe as directed.

thai-style fish
Omit the marinade. Combine 1 teaspoon shrimp paste, 1 tablespoon fish sauce, 1 seeded and finely sliced bird's eye chile, 2 cloves chopped garlic, and 1 ounce chopped ginger. Use this mixture to marinate the fish, then complete the recipe as before. Garnish with Thai basil leaves.

hot-and-spicy fish
Add 1 tablespoon hot chili paste, to taste, to the marinade ingredients, and 1 long red chile, seeded and finely sliced, to the wok with the scallions.

honey, ginger & lime shrimp

see base recipe page 184

honey, ginger & lime fish
Prepare the basic recipe, but substitute 1 pound firm, skinless white fish, de-boned and cut into bite-size pieces, for the shrimp.

soy, ginger & lime shrimp
Prepare the basic recipe, but substitute 3 tablespoons light soy sauce and 1 tablespoon sugar for the honey and fish sauce.

honey, ginger & lemongrass shrimp
Prepare the basic recipe, but omit the lime juice and zest. Add 2 tablespoons very finely chopped lemongrass to the wok with the onion and ginger.

honey, ginger & lemon calamari
Omit the shrimp and lime zest and juice from the basic recipe. Cut 1 pound calamari tubes in half lengthwise, score the insides diagonally in a diamond pattern, and slice them into strips. Complete the recipe as directed, using the calamari in place of the shrimp, and replacing the lime juice and zest with the juice and zest of 1 lemon.

pork & shrimp

see base recipe page 186

chicken & shrimp
Prepare the basic recipe, but substitute 8 ounces sliced, skinless chicken fillet for the pork fillet.

beef & shrimp
Prepare the basic recipe, but substitute 8 ounces sliced beef fillet for the pork fillet.

sweet & sour pork & shrimp
Reduce the chicken broth in the basic recipe to 1/4 cup, increase the sugar to 2 tablespoons, and combine them with the soy sauce and rice wine, also adding 1/4 cup white vinegar and 2 tablespoons of ketchup; mix well. Drain 1 (8-ounce) can of pineapple pieces, reserving 1/4 cup of the juice and mixing it with 1 tablespoon cornstarch. Prepare the recipe as directed, adding the pineapple pieces to the wok with the pork and adding the cornstarch mixture last, stirring until the sauce thickens before serving.

chili pork & shrimp
Prepare the basic recipe, adding 2 seeded and finely chopped red chiles to the wok with the curry powder, red onion, and garlic.

variations

szechuan peppercorn tuna

see base recipe page 187

szechuan peppercorn shrimp
Prepare the basic recipe, but substitute 1 pound peeled and deveined shrimp for the tuna.

black pepper & lime tuna
Omit the chili sauce, Szechuan peppercorns, and dried chiles. Prepare the basic recipe, replacing the chili sauce with the zest and juice of 1 lime, and the Szechuan peppercorns and dried chile with 2 teaspoons crushed black peppercorns.

szechuan peppercorn fish
Prepare the basic recipe, but substitute 1 pound skinless, firm white fish, de-boned and cut into bite-size pieces, for the tuna.

szechuan peppercorn & ginger tuna
Prepare the basic recipe, adding 1 ounce fresh ginger, cut into matchsticks, to the wok with the Szechuan peppercorns and dried chile.

variations

fish & vegetables

see base recipe page 188

shrimp & vegetables
Prepare the basic recipe, but substitute 1 pound peeled and deveined shrimp for the white fish.

calamari & vegetables
Prepare the basic recipe, but omit the fish. Cut 1 pound calamari tubes in half lengthwise, score the insides diagonally in a diamond pattern, and slice them into strips. Complete the recipe as directed, replacing the fish with the calamari.

fish & asian greens
Omit the carrot, red bell pepper, and broccolini from the basic recipe. Replace the carrot and pepper with 1 bunch Chinese flowering cabbage, cut into bite-size pieces, and the broccolini with 1 bunch of Chinese broccoli, cut into bite-size pieces.

fish, vegetables & chile
Prepare the basic recipe, adding 2 long red chiles, seeded and finely sliced, to the wok with the garlic and onion.

calamari with asian greens

see base recipe page 190

shrimp with asian greens
Prepare the basic recipe, but substitute 1 pound peeled and deveined shrimp for
the calamari.

calamari with ginger & asian greens
Prepare the basic recipe, adding 1 1/2 ounces fresh ginger, finely chopped, to the wok with
the garlic and scallions.

calamari with asian greens in hoisin sauce
Omit the soy sauces and sweet chili sauce. Complete the recipe as directed, adding 2/3 cup
hoisin sauce to the wok with the garlic chives.

baby octopus with asian greens
Prepare the basic recipe, but substitute 1 pound cleaned and de-beaked baby octopus for
the calamari.

lemon-pepper calamari

see base recipe page 192

garlic-pepper calamari
Prepare the basic recipe, but omit the lemon zest and juice. Replace the lemon zest and juice with 2 tablespoons hoisin sauce, and increase the garlic to 4 cloves, finely chopped.

lemon-pepper shrimp
Prepare the basic recipe, but substitute 1 pound peeled and deveined shrimp for the calamari.

lemon-pepper salmon
Prepare the basic recipe, but substitute 1 pound skinless salmon, pin-boned and cut into bite-size pieces, for the calamari.

lemon-chile calamari
Omit the black peppercorns and replace with 2 long red chiles, seeded and finely sliced, and added to the wok with the red onion and garlic.

shrimp paste & fish

see base recipe page 193

chili paste & fish
Prepare the basic recipe, but substitute 2 teaspoons chili paste, or more, to taste for the shrimp paste. Garnish the finished stir-fry with 1 finely sliced red chile.

shrimp paste & shrimp
Prepare the basic recipe, but substitute 1 pound peeled and deveined shrimp for the fish.

shrimp paste & crab
Prepare the basic recipe, but substitute 1 pound fresh crab meat for the fish.

chili paste & calamari
Omit the fish and shrimp paste from the basic recipe. Cut 1 pound calamari tubes in half lengthwise, score the insides diagonally in a diamond pattern, and slice them into strips. Follow the basic recipe, replacing the fish with the calamari, and the shrimp paste with 2 teaspoons chili paste.

singapore chili shrimp

see base recipe page 194

singapore chili crab claws
Prepare the basic recipe, but substitute 1 1/2 to 2 pounds crab claws for the shrimp.

singapore chili shrimp with noodles
Prepare 12 ounces of egg noodles according to package directions and add to the wok just after the cornstarch mixture. Complete the recipe as directed. There is no need to serve this variation with rice.

singapore chili octopus
Prepare the basic recipe, but substitute 1 1/2 pounds cleaned and de-beaked baby octopus for the shrimp.

thai chili shrimp
Omit the sauce mixture, cornstarch, and egg. Combine 1/4 cup rice wine, 3 tablespoons fish sauce, 2 tablespoons lime juice, 1 tablespoon light soy sauce, 1 tablespoon sugar, and 2 teaspoons minced lemongrass in a small bowl. Prepare the basic recipe, adding the rice wine mixture to the wok in place of the sauce mixture. Serve with fresh cilantro.

variations

shrimp with lemon & peas

see base recipe page 196

salmon with lemon & peas
Prepare the basic recipe, but substitute 1 pound skinless salmon, pin-boned and cut into bite-size pieces, for the shrimp.

calamari with lemon & peas
Prepare the basic recipe, but omit the shrimp. Cut 1 pound calamari tubes in half lengthwise, score the insides diagonally in a diamond pattern, and slice them into strips. Complete the recipe as directed, replacing the shrimp with the calamari.

shrimp with lime & peas
Prepare the basic recipe, but substitute the juice and zest of 1 lime for the lemon juice and zest.

shrimp with lemon & green beans
Prepare the basic recipe, but substitute 1 pound stringless green beans, cut into bite-size pieces for the garden and snow peas.

shrimp with lemon & bok choy
Prepare the basic recipe, but substitute 6 washed and quartered baby bok choy to the wok for the garden peas.

thai coconut fish

see base recipe page 198

thai coconut shrimp
Prepare the basic recipe, but substitute 1 pound peeled and deveined shrimp for the fish.

chili coconut fish
Prepare the basic recipe, but substitute hot chili sauce and 2 to 3 long red chiles, seeded and finely sliced, to taste, for the sweet chili sauce.

thai coconut fish & noodles
Prepare 8 ounces of dry rice noodles according to package directions and add to the wok after the 1/2 cup coconut milk. Allow them to heat through before serving.

ginger, lime & coconut fish
Prepare the basic recipe, but omit the lemongrass. Add the juice and zest of 1 lime to the fish marinade. Add 1 1/2 ounces fresh ginger, cut into matchsticks, to the wok in place of the lemongrass. Serve with lime wedges.

variations

tamarind & chile shrimp

see base recipe page 200

tamarind & chile calamari
Prepare the basic recipe, but omit the shrimp. Cut 1 pound calamari tubes in half lengthwise, score the insides diagonally in a diamond pattern, and slice them into strips. Replace the shrimp with the calamari.

tamarind & chile shrimp with thai basil
Prepare the basic recipe, adding 1 bunch of roughly chopped fresh Thai basil to the stir-fry just before serving.

tamarind & ginger shrimp
Prepare the basic recipe, but substitute 1 1/2 ounces finely chopped fresh ginger for the red chiles.

tamarind & chile shrimp with noodles
Prepare 12 ounces of egg noodles, according to package directions and add to the wok with the baby spinach. Complete the recipe as directed.

variations

sweet chili mussels with lotus root

see base recipe page 202

hot chili mussels with lotus root
Prepare the basic recipe, but halve the sweet chili sauce and increase the long red chiles to 3, seeded and finely chopped, and the chili sauce to 1/4 cup.

sweet chili octopus with lotus root
Replace the mussels with 1 pound cleaned and de-beaked baby octopus, stir-frying it until cooked instead of steaming. Complete the recipe as directed.

sweet chili mussels with water chestnuts
Omit the lotus root and splash of vinegar from the basic recipe. Add the mussels and soy sauce to the wok after stir-frying the ginger, garlic, chile, and scallions. Steam, then remove the mussels. Add 1 (16-ounce) can water chestnuts, drained, to the wok with 6 chopped baby bok choy and the sweet chili and chili sauces. Complete the recipe as directed.

sweet chili clams with lotus root
Prepare the basic recipe, but substitute 2 pounds soaked and scrubbed clams for the mussels.

variations

calamari, black bean & cucumber

see base recipe page 204

shrimp, black bean & cucumber
Prepare the basic recipe, but substitute 1 pound peeled and deveined shrimp for
the calamari.

calamari, black bean & zucchini
Prepare the basic recipe, but omit the cucumber. Add 2 medium zucchini, halved lengthwise
and sliced, to the wok with the black bean sauce.

calamari, chile & cucumber
Prepare the basic recipe, adding 2 seeded and finely sliced red chiles to the wok with the
garlic, ginger, and red onion. Complete the recipe as directed.

calamari & cucumber in hoisin sauce
Prepare the basic recipe, but substitute 2/3 cup hoisin sauce for the black bean sauce.

ginger fish

see base recipe page 206

ginger shrimp
Prepare the basic recipe, but substitute 1 pound peeled and deveined shrimp for the fish.

ginger fish with noodles
Prepare 8 ounces dry rice noodles according to package directions and add to the wok with the scallions and soy mixture. Allow them to heat through before serving. There is no need to serve this variation with rice.

garlic & chile fish
Prepare the basic recipe, but omit the ginger. Increase the garlic to 4 cloves, finely chopped, and add 3 long red chiles, seeded and finely sliced, to the wok with the onion and garlic.

ginger & basil fish
Prepare the basic recipe, but substitute 1 small bunch of basil, chopped, for the scallions.

noodles & rice

There are many varieties of noodles and rice and they form the basis of many meals. Noodles range in shape from wide and flat to thin angel hair, and are made from a range of grains, predominantly rice or wheat, sometimes with egg. They are sold fresh, frozen, dried, or in instant varieties. Rice has been a staple throughout Asia for thousands of years, and different varieties have different uses, with the longer grains most suited to stir-frying.

thai-style rice noodles (pad thai)

see variations page 260

Pad Thai is a common Thai dish that is usually sold as a street food. There are many different versions, but most contain rice noodles, tofu, eggs, tamarind, and fish sauce. It is often garnished with fried shallots and peanuts.

8 oz. dry rice stick noodles
1 tbsp. tamarind paste
1 tbsp. lime juice
2 tbsp. fish sauce
2 tbsp. coconut palm sugar or brown sugar
2 tbsp. peanut or vegetable oil
2 cloves garlic, finely chopped
1 long red chile, seeded and finely sliced
4 scallions, chopped

1 lb. peeled and deveined shrimp
8 oz. extra-firm tofu, cut into bite-size pieces
3 eggs, lightly beaten
8 oz. mung bean sprouts
1/2 cup roasted peanuts, chopped
1/2 cup fried shallots
1 small bunch fresh cilantro, chopped
lime wedges, to serve

Put the rice stick noodles in a heatproof bowl, cover completely with hot water, and let soak until tender, then drain and set aside. Combine the tamarind paste, lime juice, fish sauce, and sugar in a bowl and set aside.

Heat a wok until a drop of water evaporates in a second or two. Add the oil, garlic, chile, and scallions and stir-fry until fragrant and beginning to color. Add the shrimp and toss for 1 to 2 minutes, until the shrimp begin to change color and cook. Add the tofu, toss for 1 to 2 minutes, then make a well in the center and add the eggs. Stir-fry until nearly cooked, then add the noodles, tamarind mixture, bean sprouts, peanuts, and fried shallots and stir-fry for 1 minute more. Serve garnished with cilantro and lime wedges.

Serves 4

egg & vegetable noodles with basil

see variations page 261

Hokkien noodles are thick, yellow egg noodles that are usually sold fresh in most grocery stores. They soak up flavor and provide a great chewy texture to the finished dish.

14 oz. fresh hokkien noodles (see Glossary, page 282)

2 tbsp. peanut or vegetable oil

4 cloves garlic, finely chopped

1 oz. fresh ginger, finely chopped

1 medium red onion, halved lengthwise and sliced

1 medium red bell pepper, sliced

1 large head of broccoli, cut into bite-size florets

4 yellow squash, cut into bite-size pieces

3 eggs, lightly beaten

8 oz. snow peas, topped and tailed

8 oz. mung bean sprouts

3 tbsp. light soy sauce

2 tbsp. sweet chili sauce

3 tbsp. kecap manis (see Glossary, page 281)

1 small bunch fresh basil, chopped

Put the hokkien noodles in a heatproof bowl, cover completely with hot water, and let soak for 2 to 3 minutes, until tender. Drain and set aside.

Heat a wok until a drop of water evaporates in a second or two. Add the oil, garlic, ginger, and red onion and stir-fry until fragrant and beginning to color. Add the bell pepper and toss for 1 to 2 minutes, until it begins to soften. Add the broccoli and squash and stir-fry for 1 minute. Make a well in the center, add the eggs and stir-fry until nearly cooked. Add the snow peas, bean sprouts, noodles, soy and chili sauces, and kecap manis and stir-fry for 1 to 2 minutes. Stir in the basil and serve.

Serves 4

chinese fried rice

see variations page 262

Chinese sausage is a dried, smoked sausage made from pork with a high fat content, often seasoned with rice wine and soy sauce. It is available at most Asian grocery stores, but you can substitute pepperoni (although Chinese sausage is sweeter), chorizo, or ham.

5 tbsp. peanut or vegetable
  oil, divided
4 eggs, lightly beaten
4 cloves garlic, finely chopped
2 red chiles, seeded and
  chopped
8 oz. Chinese sausage, sliced

8 scallions, chopped
2 tbsp. rice wine
1 tsp. white sugar
1 cup garden peas, fresh
  or frozen
6 cups cooked long grain rice,
  cooled

2 tbsp. oyster sauce
1/4 cup light soy sauce
1 tbsp. sesame oil
1 long red chile, finely sliced,
  to serve

Heat a wok to medium-high heat and add 3 tablespoons peanut or vegetable oil, followed by the eggs. Swirl them around the wok to scramble them until they are just cooked. Drain the eggs on some paper towels and set aside.

Reheat the wok until a drop of water evaporates in a second or two. Add 2 tablespoons peanut or vegetable oil, garlic, and chiles and stir-fry until fragrant and beginning to color. Add the sausage and scallions and toss for 2 to 3 minutes, until the sausage has browned. Add the rice wine and sugar and stir-fry for 30 seconds. Add the peas, toss for 30 seconds, then add the rice. Gently stir-fry the rice for 1 to 2 minutes to warm it through. Add the oyster sauce, soy sauce, sesame oil, and egg to the wok. Mix gently, using the wok spatula to break the eggs into bite-size chunks, until everything is hot. Serve garnished with chile.

Serves 4

thai-style egg & pork noodles with soy (phat si-io)

see variations page 263

Chinese broccoli, also known as kai-lan or Chinese kale, is a leafy green vegetable with small, broccoli-like flowers, thick stems, and a slightly stronger flavor than regular broccoli. Broccolini is a hybrid of broccoli and Chinese broccoli, and makes a good substitute.

12 oz. dry wide rice noodles
2 tbsp. peanut or vegetable oil
4 cloves garlic, finely chopped
1 long red chile, seeded and
   finely sliced

2 long green chiles, seeded
   and finely sliced
1 lb. pork fillet, thinly sliced
1 large bunch Chinese
   broccoli, chopped
3 eggs, lightly beaten

3 tbsp. dark soy sauce
2 tbsp. light soy sauce
3 tbsp. oyster sauce
1 tsp. coconut palm sugar or
   brown sugar
1/4 cup water, if needed

Put the rice noodles in a heatproof bowl and cover completely with hot water. Soak the noodles until tender, then drain and set aside.

Heat a wok until a drop of water evaporates in a second or two. Add the oil, garlic, and chiles, and stir-fry until fragrant and beginning to color. Add the pork, tossing for 1 to 2 minutes, until it begins to cook.

Add the Chinese broccoli and stir-fry for a minute. Make a well in the center and add the eggs. Stir-fry until nearly cooked, then add the noodles, both soy sauces, oyster sauce, and sugar, and stir-fry for 1 minute, adding water if needed, then serve.

Serves 4

thai-style chicken fried rice (khao pad)

see variations page 264

Khao pad is a Thai version of fried rice. It uses jasmine rice, and often contains eggs, meat, onions, and garlic. Fried rice is a great way of using up leftover steamed rice, and works best with rice that has been cooked, cooled quickly, and refrigerated.

3 tbsp. peanut or vegetable oil
4 cloves garlic, finely chopped
2 Thai red chiles, seeded and chopped
1 lb. skinless chicken thighs, cut into
   bite-size pieces
8 scallions, chopped
6 cups cooked jasmine rice, cooled
3 eggs

1/4 cup light soy sauce
3 tbsp. fish sauce
1 tbsp. lime juice
1 tbsp. coconut palm sugar or brown sugar
1 small bunch fresh cilantro, chopped
soy or chili sauce, to serve
lime wedges, to serve

Heat a wok until a drop of water evaporates in a second or two. Add the oil, garlic, and chiles, and stir-fry until fragrant and beginning to color. Add the chicken and scallions, tossing for 2 to 3 minutes, until the chicken is nearly cooked.

Add the rice and stir-fry for 1 to 2 minutes. Make a well in the center and add the eggs. Stir the eggs until they are almost set, then mix them into the rice. Add the soy sauce, fish sauce, lime juice, and sugar and stir-fry for 2 to 3 minutes, until the chicken is cooked. Gently mix the cilantro through the stir-fry. Serve with extra soy or chili sauce and lime wedges.

Serves 4

indonesian-style fried rice (nasi goreng)

see variations page 265

Also popular in Malaysia and Singapore, this rice dish generally contains chicken, shrimp, and eggs flavored with sweet soy (kecap manis). Kecap manis can be found in the Asian section of grocery stores, specialty stores, or online.

5–6 tbsp. peanut or
  vegetable oil, divided
4 cloves garlic, finely chopped
8 scallions, chopped
1 tsp. shrimp paste (see
  Glossary, page 282)
4 oz. bacon, chopped

8 oz. skinless chicken thigh,
  thinly sliced
1 stalk celery, thinly sliced
6 cups cooked rice, cooled
8 oz. cooked small shrimp
8 oz. mung bean sprouts
1/4 cup kecap manis

2 tbsp. light soy sauce
4 eggs
1 small bunch fresh cilantro,
  chopped, to serve
1/2 cup fried shallots, to serve
soy sauce, extra, to serve
fresh red chile, sliced, to serve

Heat a wok until a drop of water evaporates in a second or two. Add 3 tablespoons oil, garlic, scallions, and shrimp paste and stir-fry until fragrant and beginning to color. Add the bacon and toss for 1 to 2 minutes until the bacon starts to cook and color. Add the chicken and celery, and stir-fry until almost cooked.

Add the rice and gently stir-fry for 1 to 2 minutes. Add the cooked shrimp, bean sprouts, kecap manis, and soy sauce to the wok and stir-fry for 2 to 3 minutes more, until the chicken is cooked and the rice is hot. Transfer the fried rice to a serving dish, cover, and keep warm while cooking the eggs.

Heat a large skillet, add 2 to 3 tablespoons oil, and carefully add the eggs. Fry the eggs until the whites are set and the yolks are still soft, or to your preference. Plate four portions of fried rice and top each serving with a fried egg, cilantro, and fried shallots, and serve with extra soy sauce and sliced chile.

Serves 4

pork & shrimp with hokkien noodles (hokkien mee)

see variations page 266

Hokkien mee is a dish that originated in the Fujian (Hokkien) province of China. It often contains pork, lard, eggs, and seafood stir-fried with egg noodles and rice noodles. The noodles are cooked in the wok, soaking up the broth and sauces.

2 tbsp. peanut or vegetable oil
4 cloves garlic, finely chopped
1 lb. pork shoulder, finely sliced
8 oz. peeled and deveined shrimp
1/4 small Chinese cabbage, cut into
    bite-size pieces

1/4 cup dark soy sauce
2 tbsp. light soy sauce
2 tbsp. oyster sauce
1 lb. fresh hokkien noodles
1 cup chicken broth

Heat a wok until a drop of water evaporates in a second or two. Add the oil and garlic and stir-fry until fragrant and beginning to color. Add the pork, tossing for 2 to 3 minutes, until it begins to color and cook.

Add the shrimp and stir-fry for a minute, then add the Chinese cabbage and stir-fry until nearly cooked. Add the dark soy sauce, light soy sauce, oyster sauce, noodles, and chicken broth and simmer for 2 to 3 minutes, until the noodles and cabbage are tender. Serve immediately.

Serves 4

seafood fried rice

see variations page 267

A mix of fresh seafood is perfect for fried rice, and you can use whatever is available. Planning ahead by cooking the rice the day before and refrigerating it overnight will give the best results.

3 tbsp. peanut or vegetable oil
4 cloves garlic, finely chopped
1 oz. fresh ginger, finely chopped
8 scallions, chopped
8 oz. peeled and deveined shrimp
4 oz. calamari rings
4 oz. fresh scallop meat
4 oz. fresh crab meat

6 cups cooked long grain rice, cooled
3 eggs
8 oz. mung bean sprouts
1/4 cup light soy sauce
2 tbsp. fish sauce
soy sauce, to serve
lemon wedges, to serve

Heat a wok until a drop of water evaporates in a second or two. Add the oil, garlic, ginger, and scallions and stir-fry until fragrant and beginning to color. Add the shrimp, tossing for 1 to 2 minutes, until the shrimp have started to change color. Add the calamari, scallop meat, and crab meat and stir-fry until almost cooked.

Add the rice and gently stir-fry for 1 to 2 minutes. Make a well in the center of the rice and add the eggs into the well. Stir the eggs until they are almost set, then mix them into the rice. Add the bean sprouts, soy sauce, and fish sauce and stir-fry for 2 to 3 minutes, until the seafood is cooked and the rice hot. Serve with extra soy sauce and lemon wedges.

Serves 4

egg fried rice with chile & peas

see variations page 268

Egg fried rice is a versatile side dish or a meal on its own. This recipe uses peas, but any finely chopped vegetable you have to hand could be added to this super-easy recipe.

3 tbsp. peanut or vegetable oil
4 cloves garlic, finely chopped
2 red chiles, seeded and chopped
8 scallions, chopped
2 cups garden peas, fresh or frozen

6 cups cooked long grain rice, cooled
1/4 cup light soy sauce
4 eggs, lightly beaten
1 tsp. sesame oil
1 long red chile, finely sliced, to serve

Heat a wok until a drop of water evaporates in a second or two. Add the oil, garlic, and chiles and stir-fry until fragrant and beginning to color. Add the scallions and peas and toss in the wok for 1 to 2 minutes.

Add the rice and gently stir-fry for 1 to 2 minutes to warm it through. Add the soy sauce to the wok and mix gently. Make a well in the center of the rice and add the eggs to the well. Stir the eggs until they are almost set, then mix them into the rice, cooking until everything is hot and combined. Serve garnished with chile slices.

Serves 4

green curry noodles

see variations page 269

Curry pastes are made from a selection of herbs and spices, usually blended with oil and salt, and they provide a wonderful base flavor for many dishes. A variety of commercial curry pastes are available, packaged in jars; look for them in Asian grocers or the Asian food aisle of the grocery store.

2 tbsp. peanut or vegetable oil
1 clove garlic, finely chopped
1 large red onion, halved lengthwise, and sliced
2 tbsp. green curry paste
1 lb. extra-firm tofu, cut into bite-size pieces
1 large carrot, sliced

1 red bell pepper, sliced
4 baby bok choy, cut into bite-size pieces
2 tbsp. light soy sauce
1 lb. fresh hokkien noodles
1 cup coconut milk

Heat a wok until a drop of water evaporates in a second or two. Add the oil, garlic, red onion, and curry paste and stir-fry until fragrant and beginning to color. Add the tofu and toss gently for 2 to 3 minutes, until it begins to color and cook.

Add the carrot and bell pepper and stir-fry for 1 to 2 minutes. Add the bok choy, light soy sauce, noodles, and coconut milk and simmer for 2 to 3 minutes, until the noodles and bok choy are just tender. Serve immediately.

Serves 4

shrimp, ginger & mushroom fried rice

see variations page 270

Fried shallots are finely sliced shallots that have been deep fried until brown and crisp. They are an essential condiment in a lot of Vietnamese cooking, lending a sweet, salty flavor and crunch to finished dishes. They can be found at Asian grocery stores.

3 tbsp. peanut or vegetable oil
2 cloves garlic, finely chopped
1 1/2 oz. fresh ginger, finely chopped
4 scallions, chopped
8 oz. button mushrooms, sliced
1 lb. peeled and deveined shrimp
6 cups cooked rice, cooled

4 oz. baby spinach
2 tsp. sesame oil
2 tbsp. oyster sauce
1/4 cup light soy sauce
1/2 cup fried shallots, to serve
lemon wedges, to serve

Heat a wok until a drop of water evaporates in a second or two. Add the oil, garlic, ginger, and scallions and stir-fry until fragrant and beginning to color. Add the mushrooms and stir-fry for 1 to 2 minutes, until they start to soften and color. Add the shrimp and toss until colored and almost cooked.

Add the rice and gently stir-fry for 1 to 2 minutes. Add the baby spinach, sesame oil, oyster sauce, and soy sauce and stir-fry for 2 to 3 minutes, until the shrimp are cooked and the rice is hot. Serve with fried shallots and lemon wedges.

Serves 4

turkey & fried brown rice with ginger & cilantro

see variations page 271

Brown rice is higher in fiber than white rice and takes about three times longer to cook, so take that into account when preparing this dish. Pre-cooking the rice the day before and cooling in the refrigerator overnight can substantially cut preparation times.

2 tbsp. peanut or vegetable oil
1 small bunch cilantro, leaves removed, and
    stems and roots (if available) finely chopped
2 cloves garlic, peeled and finely chopped
1 1/2 oz. fresh ginger, finely chopped
8 scallions, chopped
1 lb. ground turkey

6 cups cooked long-grain brown rice, cooled
8 oz. tatsoi leaves (see Glossary, page 280)
8 oz. mung bean sprouts
1/4 cup light soy sauce
1 tbsp. kecap manis
1 tsp. sesame oil

Heat a wok until a drop of water evaporates in a second or two. Add the oil, finely chopped cilantro stems and roots, garlic, ginger, and scallions and stir-fry until fragrant and beginning to color. Add the turkey and toss for 3 to 4 minutes, breaking up any lumps, until golden and cooked.

Add the rice and gently stir-fry for 1 to 2 minutes to warm it through. Add the tatsoi, bean sprouts, soy sauce, kecap manis, and sesame oil and stir-fry until everything is combined and hot. Toss through half the cilantro leaves. Serve garnished with the remaining cilantro leaves.

Serves 4

beef & cabbage with udon noodles

see variations page 272

This recipe uses Chinese cabbage, also known as wombok and napa cabbage, among other names. It is an elongated cabbage with white stems and pale green leaves, with a mild flavor. If unavailable, use regular cabbage, and lengthen cooking times slightly.

1 lb. fresh udon noodles (see Glossary,
    page 282)
2 tbsp. peanut or vegetable oil
4 cloves garlic, finely chopped
1 oz. fresh ginger, finely chopped
1 large yellow onion, halved lengthwise,
    and sliced

1 lb. beef sirloin, sliced
1/2 small Chinese cabbage, cut into
    bite-size pieces
3 tbsp. light soy sauce
3 tbsp. kecap manis
1/4 cup water
1 small bunch Thai basil, chopped

Put the udon noodles in a heatproof bowl, cover completely with hot water, and let soak for 2 to 3 minutes, until tender. Drain the noodles and set aside.

Heat a wok until a drop of water evaporates in a second or two. Add the oil, garlic, ginger, and onion, and stir-fry until fragrant and beginning to color. Add the beef to the wok and toss for 1 to 2 minutes, until it changes color and begins to cook.

Add the Chinese cabbage and stir-fry until nearly tender, then add the noodles, light soy sauce, kecap manis, and water and stir-fry for 1 to 2 minutes. Toss the chopped Thai basil through the stir-fry before serving.

Serves 4

broccoli, tofu & sweet soy noodles

see variations page 273

This recipe uses packaged fresh egg noodles, which can be briefly boiled or soaked before using, or, as they are in this recipe, added directly to the wok with a little extra liquid. Prepared this way, they cook with the other ingredients, soaking up plenty of flavor. A specialty soy sauce called kecap manis adds its distinctive sweetness to this dish.

2 tbsp. peanut or vegetable oil
2 cloves garlic, finely chopped
1 oz. fresh ginger, finely chopped
1 medium yellow onion, halved lengthwise,
    and chopped
1 lb. extra-firm tofu, cut into bite-size pieces

2 medium heads broccoli, cut into
    bite-size florets
1/3 cup kecap manis
2 tbsp. light soy sauce
12 oz. fresh, thick egg noodles
1/2 cup vegetable broth

Heat a wok until a drop of water evaporates in a second or two. Add the oil, garlic, ginger, and onion and stir-fry until fragrant and beginning to color. Add the tofu, tossing for 2 to 3 minutes, until it begins to color and cook.

Add the broccoli and stir-fry for 1 to 2 minutes, then add the kecap manis, light soy sauce, noodles, and vegetable broth and simmer for 2 to 3 minutes, tossing occasionally, until the noodles and broccoli are just tender. Serve immediately.

Serves 4

tempeh & rice noodles with chile

see variations page 274

Rice noodles come in many widths, from very fine angel hair (vermicelli) to 1/2-inch (1.25-cm) wide noodles, and wider. If available, you can use fresh rice noodles for this recipe, adding them straight to the wok with a little extra liquid.

8 oz. dry wide rice noodles
3 tbsp. peanut or vegetable oil
2 cloves garlic, finely chopped
2 long red chiles, seeded and finely sliced
1 long green chile, seeded and finely sliced
6 scallions, chopped
1 lb. tempeh, cut into bite-size pieces
    (see Glossary, page 282)

2 medium zucchini, halved lengthwise and sliced
1 (8-oz.) can baby corn, drained
4 baby bok choy, chopped
2 tbsp. dark soy sauce
3 tbsp. light soy sauce
2 tbsp. sweet chili sauce
2–3 tbsp. water, if needed
1 small bunch fresh cilantro, chopped

Put the rice noodles into a heatproof bowl, cover completely with hot water, and let soak until tender. Drain and set aside.

Heat a wok until a drop of water evaporates in a second or two. Add the oil, garlic, chiles, and scallions and stir-fry until fragrant and beginning to color. Add the tempeh, tossing for 1 to 2 minutes, until it begins to color and cook. Add the zucchini and stir-fry until nearly cooked, then add the baby corn, bok choy, noodles, dark and light soy sauces, and sweet chili sauce. Stir-fry for 2 to 3 minutes, adding a little water if needed, until the bok choy is crisp-tender and the noodles are hot. Serve garnished with cilantro.

Serves 4

vietnamese-style beef with rice vermicelli

see variations page 275

Rice vermicelli are also known as angel hair rice noodles. They are the thinnest rice noodles available. They will only need to soak in hot water for a few minutes to soften enough to use.

2 cloves garlic, finely chopped
1 oz. fresh ginger, finely sliced
1 long red chile, seeded and finely sliced
2 tbsp. oyster sauce
2 tbsp. light soy sauce
1 tbsp. lime juice
1 tbsp. fish sauce

2 tsp. coconut palm sugar or brown sugar
1 tbsp. cornstarch
1 lb. beef sirloin, thinly sliced
12 oz. dry vermicelli rice noodles
2 tbsp. peanut or vegetable oil
2 carrots, sliced

1 large red onion, halved lengthwise, and sliced
2 stalks celery, sliced
1/4 cup water
1/2 cup roasted peanuts, chopped
1 small bunch Vietnamese mint, chopped (see Glossary, page 282)

Combine the garlic, ginger, chile, oyster sauce, light soy sauce, lime juice, fish sauce, sugar, cornstarch, and beef in a bowl and mix well. Set aside to marinate for 15 minutes. Put the rice noodles into a heatproof bowl, cover completely with hot water, and let soak until tender. Drain the noodles and set aside.

Heat a wok until a drop of water evaporates in a second or two. Add the oil, carrots, red onion, and celery and stir-fry until fragrant and beginning to color. Add the beef and marinade to the wok and toss for 1 to 2 minutes, until the beef begins to cook.

Add the noodles and water and stir-fry until the beef is cooked and the noodles are hot, adding extra water if needed. Serve the stir-fry sprinkled with the roasted peanuts and Vietnamese mint.

Serves 4

pork chow mein

see variations page 276

Chow mein is a stir-fried noodle dish that is very popular throughout China and the West. There are many different versions of this dish, depending on where it is prepared, and it can be easily adjusted to use what you have on hand.

2 tbsp. peanut or vegetable oil
2 cloves garlic, finely chopped
8 scallions, chopped
1 lb. ground pork
1 lb. fresh chow mein noodles
1 large carrot, sliced
1 red bell pepper, sliced

1 cup fresh or frozen garden peas
1/4 small Chinese cabbage, shredded
2 tsp. cornstarch
1/2 cup chicken broth
3 tbsp. light soy sauce
1/4 cup oyster sauce

Heat a wok until a drop of water evaporates in a second or two. Add the oil, garlic, and scallions and stir-fry until fragrant and beginning to color. Add the pork and toss, breaking up any lumps, until just cooked. Add the noodles, frying until they start to become crisp.

Add the carrot and bell pepper and stir-fry until nearly tender, then add the peas and Chinese cabbage. Combine the cornstarch and chicken broth and add to the wok with the light soy sauce and oyster sauce. Stir immediately to prevent lumps from forming. Bring to a simmer, then stir-fry until the vegetables are crisp-tender and the sauce has thickened. Serve immediately.

Serves 4

japanese-style chicken & noodles

see variations page 277

Mirin is a sweet rice wine from Japan; it can be found in the Asian section of grocery stores. If it is unavailable, substitute it with 1/4 cup dry white wine or sherry mixed with 2 teaspoons of sugar.

1 lb. udon noodles
1/4 cup light soy sauce
1/4 cup mirin
1 tsp. sesame oil
1 tbsp. white sugar
1/4 tsp. red pepper flakes

2 tbsp. peanut or vegetable oil
2 cloves garlic, peeled and finely chopped
6 scallions, chopped
1 lb. skinless chicken fillet, sliced
1/4 small green cabbage, shredded
8 oz. snow peas, topped and tailed

Put the udon noodles in a heatproof bowl and cover completely with hot water. Let soak for 2 to 3 minutes, until tender, then drain and set aside. Combine the light soy sauce, mirin, sesame oil, sugar, and red pepper flakes in a bowl and set aside.

Heat a wok until a drop of water evaporates in a second or two. Add the peanut or vegetable oil, garlic, and scallions and stir-fry until fragrant and beginning to color. Add the chicken and toss for 1 to 2 minutes until it changes color and begins to cook.

Add the cabbage and stir-fry until nearly tender, then add the snow peas, noodles, and soy sauce mixture and stir-fry for 1 to 2 minutes, until the noodles are hot and the vegetables are crisp-tender. Serve immediately.

Serves 4

chicken & shrimp with egg noodles & basil

see variations page 278

Fresh ginger and garlic give this recipe a fantastic flavor. They are readily available in most grocery stores, but they can also be purchased ready-minced in jars for convenience. Follow the directions on the jar for the amount to use in place of fresh.

2 tbsp. peanut or vegetable oil
2 cloves garlic, finely chopped
1 oz. fresh ginger, finely chopped
1 large red onion, halved lengthwise, and chopped
8 oz. skinless chicken thigh, sliced
8 oz. peeled and deveined shrimp

1 green bell pepper, cut into bite-size pieces
1/2 small cauliflower, cut into bite-size pieces
3 tbsp. light soy sauce
2 tbsp. kecap manis
1 lb. fresh hokkien noodles
1/2 cup water
1 small bunch fresh basil, chopped

Heat a wok until a drop of water evaporates in a second or two. Add the oil, garlic, ginger, and red onion and stir-fry until fragrant and beginning to color. Add the chicken, tossing for 2 to 3 minutes, until it begins to color and cook.

Add the shrimp and stir-fry for 1 to 2 minutes until they change color. Add the bell pepper and cauliflower and stir-fry for 1 to 2 minutes. Add the light soy sauce, kecap manis, noodles, and water and toss for 2 to 3 minutes, until the noodles and vegetables are just tender, adding more water if required. Toss the chopped basil through the stir-fry and serve immediately.

Serves 4

vegetables & egg noodles (vegetable lo mein)

see variations page 279

Lo mein and chow mein can be quite similar in execution, but the difference generally lies in the noodles — chow mein noodles are fried in the wok to crisp up, whereas lo mein noodles are softer, because they are added to the sauce in the wok.

1 lb. fresh thin egg noodles
2 tbsp. peanut or vegetable oil
2 cloves garlic, finely chopped
4 scallions, chopped
8 shitake mushrooms, sliced
8 button mushrooms, sliced
1 carrot, sliced

1 yellow bell pepper, sliced
8 oz. green beans, topped and tailed
8 oz. snow peas, topped and tailed
1 tbsp. Chinese rice wine
1 tsp. coconut palm sugar or brown sugar
1/4 cup light soy sauce
2 tbsp. dark soy sauce

Put the egg noodles in a heatproof bowl, cover completely with hot water, and let soak for 1 to 2 minutes, until tender. Drain and set aside.

Heat a wok until a drop of water evaporates in a second or two. Add the oil, garlic, and scallions and stir-fry until fragrant and beginning to color. Add both types of mushroom and toss in the wok until they have started to soften and cook. Add the carrot and bell pepper and stir-fry for 1 to 2 minutes, until they begin to soften.

Add the green beans and stir-fry for a minute, then add the snow peas, rice wine, sugar, noodles, light soy sauce, and dark soy sauce, and stir-fry for 1 to 2 minutes, until the vegetables are crisp-tender. Serve immediately.

Serves 4

variations

thai-style rice noodles (pad thai)

see base recipe page 229

chicken pad thai
Prepare the basic recipe, but substitute 1 pound skinless chicken fillet, cut into bite-size pieces, for the shrimp.

pork pad thai
Prepare the basic recipe, but substitute 1 pound sliced pork fillet for the shrimp.

vegetarian pad thai
Prepare the basic recipe, but omit the fish sauce and shrimp. Replace the fish sauce with soy sauce, and increase the tofu to 1 pound, adding it to the wok after the scallions. Complete the recipe as directed.

calamari pad thai
Prepare the basic recipe, but omit the shrimp. Cut 1 pound calamari tubes in half lengthwise, score the insides diagonally in a diamond pattern, and slice them into strips and use in place of the calamari.

egg & vegetable noodles with basil

see base recipe page 230

egg & vegetable noodles with chile
Prepare the basic recipe, but omit the basil. Add 2 seeded and finely sliced red chiles to the wok with the garlic, ginger, and red onion.

chile & vegetable noodles with basil
Prepare the basic recipe, but omit the eggs. Add 2 seeded and finely sliced red chiles to the wok with the garlic, ginger, and red onion.

chicken & vegetable noodles with basil
Prepare the basic recipe, but omit the eggs. Add 1 pound sliced, skinless chicken fillet to the wok after the garlic, ginger, and red onion.

shrimp & vegetable noodles with egg
Prepare the basic recipe, but omit the basil. Add 1 pound peeled and deveined shrimp to the wok after the garlic, ginger, and red onion.

variations

chinese fried rice

see base recipe page 232

curry fried rice
Omit the Chinese sausage, peas, and oyster sauce from the basic recipe. Replace the Chinese sausage with 8 ounces chopped ham, and add 1 tablespoon curry powder to the wok with the ham and scallions. Complete the recipe as directed, replacing the peas with 2 chopped carrots.

american-style fried rice
Omit the Chinese sausage, peas, and oyster sauce from the basic recipe. Replace the Chinese sausage with 8 ounces chopped bacon, the peas with 2 chopped tomatoes, and the oyster sauce with 2 tablespoons of ketchup.

hawaiian-style fried rice
Omit the Chinese sausage and peas from the basic recipe. Replace the Chinese sausage with 8 ounces chopped ham and the peas with 1 (8-ounce) can of pineapple pieces, drained.

special fried rice
Prepare the basic recipe, reducing the Chinese sausage by half, and adding 4 ounces shredded roast chicken and 4 ounces cooked, shelled shrimp to the wok with the peas.

thai-style egg & pork noodles with soy (phat si-io)

see base recipe page 234

malaysian-style egg & pork noodles with soy (char kway teow)
Omit the Chinese broccoli from the basic recipe. Add 6 chopped scallions and 1 teaspoon shrimp paste to the wok with the garlic and chiles. Complete the recipe as directed, replacing the Chinese broccoli with 1 pound bean sprouts.

phat si-io with beef
Prepare the basic recipe, but substitute 1 pound thinly sliced beef fillet for the pork.

phat si-io with shrimp
Prepare the basic recipe, but substitute 1 pound peeled and deveined shrimp for the pork.

phat si-io with chicken
Prepare the basic recipe, but substitute 1 pound thinly sliced chicken fillet for the pork.

variations

thai-style chicken fried rice (khao pad)

see base recipe page 235

thai style shrimp fried rice
Prepare the basic recipe, but substitute 1 pound peeled and deveined shrimp for the chicken.

thai style vegetarian fried rice
Omit the chicken and fish sauce from the basic recipe. Replace the chicken with 1 pound extra-firm tofu, chopped, and the fish sauce with extra soy sauce, to taste.

thai style pork fried rice
Prepare the basic recipe, but substitute 1 pound pork fillet, cut into bite-size pieces, for the chicken.

thai style crab fried rice
Prepare the basic recipe, but substitute 1 pound fresh crab meat for the chicken. Complete the recipe as directed, taking care not to over-cook the crab meat by removing it from the wok before adding the rice, and adding it back toward the end of cooking.

indonesian-style fried rice (nasi goreng)

see base recipe page 236

nasi goreng with tomato & chili
Prepare the basic recipe, adding 2 long red chiles, seeded and finely chopped, to the wok with the garlic and scallions. Add 2 large, chopped tomatoes to the wok with the shrimp and bean sprouts.

nasi goreng with beef
Prepare the basic recipe, but substitute 8 ounces finely sliced beef fillet for the chicken.

nasi goreng with seafood
Omit the chicken from the basic recipe. Prepare the recipe as directed, adding 8 ounces skinless, boneless firm white fish, cut into bite-size pieces, to the wok in place of the chicken, and 4 ounces cooked crab meat to the wok with the shrimp.

vegetarian nasi goring
Omit the shrimp paste, chicken, bacon, and shrimp from the basic recipe. Replace the bacon and chicken with 12 ounces extra-firm tofu, cut into bite-size pieces. Complete the recipe as directed, adding 3 chopped baby bok choy to the wok with the bean sprouts.

nasi goreng with mushroom
Prepare the basic recipe as directed, adding 2 large, sliced portobello mushrooms to the wok with the chicken and celery.

variations

pork & shrimp with hokkien noodles (hokkien mee)

see base recipe page 238

hokkien mee with fish cakes
Prepare the basic recipe, but substitute 8 ounces of sliced fish cakes for the shrimp.
Fish cakes can be found in most Asian grocers, in the freezer section.

vegetarian hokkien mee
Omit the pork, shrimp, and oyster sauce from the basic recipe. Replace the pork with
1 pound extra-firm tofu, cut into bite-size pieces, and the shrimp with 8 ounces sliced
button mushrooms. Complete the recipe as directed.

chicken hokkien mee
Prepare the basic recipe, but substitute 1 pound thinly sliced, skinless chicken thigh for
the pork.

spicy hokkien mee
Prepare the basic recipe as directed, adding 2 seeded and finely sliced red chiles to the wok
with the garlic and 2 to 3 teaspoons chili sauce, to taste, to the wok with the chicken broth.

seafood fried rice

see base recipe page 240

fish fried rice
Prepare the basic recipe, but substitute 1 pound firm, skinless and boneless fish cut into bite-size pieces for the shrimp, calamari, scallop meat, and crab meat.

seafood fried rice with chili & basil
Prepare the basic recipe, but add 2 seeded and finely sliced red chiles to the wok with the garlic, ginger, and scallions. Complete the recipe as directed, adding a small bunch of chopped fresh basil to the wok just before serving.

seafood fried rice with snow peas
Prepare the basic recipe, but substitute 8 ounces snow peas, topped and tailed and roughly chopped, for the bean sprouts.

seafood fried rice with fish cakes
Prepare the basic recipe, but substitute 8 ounces sliced fish cakes for the scallop meat and crab meat.

variations

egg fried rice with chile & peas

see base recipe page 241

egg fried rice with shrimp & peas
Prepare the basic recipe, adding 8 ounces small, cooked shrimp to the wok with the rice. Complete the recipe as directed.

egg fried rice with peas & sambal
Prepare the basic recipe, adding 2 to 3 teaspoons sambal oelek, to taste, to the wok with the scallions and peas. Complete the recipe as directed.

egg fried brown rice with chile & peas
Prepare the basic recipe, but substitute 6 cups of cooked and cooled long grain brown rice for the long grain rice.

egg fried rice with lemon & peas
Prepare the basic recipe, but omit the finely chopped red chile. Complete the recipe as directed and add 1 tablespoon finely chopped lemongrass to the wok with the garlic and 2 tablespoons lemon juice and 1 teaspoon sugar to the wok with the soy sauce. Serve with lemon wedges.

green curry noodles

see base recipe page 242

red curry noodles
Prepare the basic recipe, but substitute 2 tablespoons red curry paste for the green
curry paste.

yellow curry noodles
Prepare the basic recipe, but substitute 2 tablespoons yellow curry paste for the green
curry paste.

green curry noodles with chicken
Prepare the basic recipe, but substitute 1 pound thinly sliced, skinless chicken thighs for
the tofu.

green curry noodles with shrimp
Prepare the basic recipe, but substitute 1 pound of peeled and deveined shrimp for the tofu.

variations

shrimp, ginger & mushroom fried rice

see base recipe page 244

shrimp, ginger & broccoli fried rice

Prepare the basic recipe, but omit the mushrooms. Add the shrimp to the wok after the garlic, ginger, and scallions, and stir-fry for 1 to 2 minutes. Add 2 medium-size heads of broccoli, cut into bite-size florets, and stir-fry for 1 to 2 minutes. Complete the recipe as directed.

shrimp, garlic & mushroom fried rice

Omit the ginger from the basic recipe and increase the garlic to 4 cloves.

calamari, ginger & mushroom fried rice

Prepare the basic recipe, but omit the shrimp. Cut 1 pound calamari tubes in half lengthwise, score the insides diagonally in a diamond pattern, and slice them into strips. Replace the shrimp with the calamari.

shrimp, ginger & water chestnut fried rice

Reduce the mushrooms in the basic recipe by half. Prepare the recipe as directed, adding 2 (8-ounce) cans of drained water chestnuts to the wok with the baby spinach.

variations

turkey & fried brown rice with ginger & cilantro

see base recipe page 246

pork & fried brown rice with ginger & cilantro
Prepare the basic recipe, but substitute 1 pound ground pork for the ground turkey.

chicken & fried brown rice with ginger & cilantro
Prepare the basic recipe, but substitute 1 pound ground chicken for the ground turkey.

turkey & fried brown rice with ginger & garlic
Omit the cilantro from the basic recipe and increase the garlic to 4 cloves, finely chopped.

turkey & fried brown rice with chili & cilantro
Reduce the ginger in the basic recipe to 1 ounce. Complete the recipe as directed, adding
2 seeded and finely chopped red chiles to the wok with the garlic, ginger, and scallions. Serve
with extra finely sliced red chile.

beef & cabbage with udon noodles

see base recipe page 247

chicken & cabbage with udon noodles
Prepare the basic recipe, but substitute 1 pound sliced skinless chicken fillet for the beef.

beef & red bell pepper with udon noodles
Prepare the basic recipe, but substitute 3 red bell peppers, sliced, for the Chinese cabbage.

shrimp & bok choy with udon noodles
Omit the beef and Chinese cabbage from the basic recipe. Prepare the recipe as directed, replacing the beef with 1 pound peeled and deveined shrimp, and the Chinese cabbage with 8 baby bok choy, cut into bite-size pieces.

vegetables with udon noodles
Prepare the basic recipe, but substitute 1 sliced medium carrot and 1 sliced large red bell pepper for the beef. Complete the recipe as directed, adding 8 ounces of bean sprouts to the wok with the Chinese cabbage.

variations

broccoli, tofu & sweet soy noodles

see base recipe page 248

broccoli, tofu & sweet soy noodles with egg
Prepare the basic recipe as directed and transfer the noodles to a covered serving dish to keep warm. Heat a skillet, add 2 tablespoons oil, and carefully add 4 eggs. Fry the eggs until the whites are set and the yolks still soft, or to your preference. Serve the noodles, topping each serving with an egg.

broccoli, tofu & sweet soy noodles with chile
Prepare the basic recipe as directed, adding 2 long red chiles, seeded and finely sliced, to the wok with the garlic, ginger, and onion.

broccoli, mushroom & sweet soy noodles
Prepare the basic recipe, but substitute 1 pound sliced mushrooms for the tofu.

chinese cabbage, tofu & sweet soy noodles
Prepare the basic recipe, but substitute 1/2 a small Chinese cabbage, cut into bite-size pieces, for the broccoli.

tempeh & rice noodles with chile

see base recipe page 250

tofu & rice noodles with chile
Prepare the basic recipe, but substitute 1 pound extra-firm tofu, cut into bite-size pieces, for the tempeh.

green vegetables & rice noodles with chile
Prepare the basic recipe, but substitute 1 large head of broccoli, cut into bite-size florets, for the tempeh. Add 4 ounces baby spinach to the stir-fry just before serving.

tempeh & egg noodles with chile
Omit the rice noodles from the basic recipe. Soak 1 pound egg noodles in hot water for 2 to 3 minutes, drain, and use in place of the rice noodles.

tempeh & rice noodle with sambal
Prepare the basic recipe, but substitute 1 to 2 tablespoons sambal oelek, to taste, for the chiles.

vietnamese-style beef with rice vermicelli

see base recipe page 252

vietnamese-style chicken with rice vermicelli
Prepare the basic recipe, but substitute 1 pound sliced, skinless chicken thigh for the beef.

vietnamese-style lemongrass beef with rice vermicelli
Add 1 stalk lemongrass, outer leaves and root discarded, white part finely chopped, to the beef mixture. Complete the recipe as directed.

vietnamese-style beef with rice vermicelli & chile
Prepare the basic recipe, adding 2 seeded and finely sliced red chiles to the wok with the onion, carrots, and celery. Serve with extra sliced red chili.

vietnamese-style tofu with rice vermicelli
Prepare the basic recipe, but substitute 1 pound extra-firm tofu, cut into bite-size pieces, for the beef.

variations

pork chow mein

see base recipe page 254

chicken chow mein
Prepare the basic recipe, but substitute 1 pound ground chicken for the ground pork.

shrimp chow mein
Prepare the basic recipe, but substitute 1 pound peeled, deveined, and chopped shrimp meat for the ground pork.

vegetarian chow mein
Omit the ground pork, oyster sauce, and chicken broth from the basic recipe. Complete the recipe as directed, replacing the pork with 1 pound chopped extra-firm tofu; the oyster sauce with 1/4 cup black bean sauce; and the chicken broth with 1/2 cup vegetable broth.

beef chow mein
Prepare the basic recipe, but substitute 1 pound ground beef for the ground pork.

japanese-style chicken & noodles

see base recipe page 255

japanese-style beef & noodles
Prepare the basic recipe, but substitute 1 pound sliced beef sirloin for the chicken.

japanese-style shrimp & noodles
Prepare the basic recipe, but substitute 1 pound peeled and deveined shrimp for the chicken.

japanese-style tofu & noodles
Prepare the basic recipe, but substitute 1 pound extra-firm tofu, cut into bite-size pieces, for the chicken.

spicy chicken & noodles
Complete the recipe as directed, but increase the red pepper flakes to 1 to 2 teaspoons, to taste, and add 1 to 2 tablespoons chili sauce to the sauce mixture.

variations

chicken & shrimp with egg noodles & basil

see base recipe page 256

chicken & shrimp with egg noodles & cashews
Prepare the basic recipe, but substitute 2/3 cup of roasted cashews, tossed through the stir-fry just before serving, for the basil.

turkey & shrimp with egg noodles & basil
Prepare the basic recipe, but substitute 8 ounces turkey breast, cut into bite-size pieces, for the chicken.

chicken & shrimp with rice vermicelli
Omit the egg noodles from the basic recipe. Put 12 ounces rice vermicelli into a bowl, cover with hot water, soak until tender, then drain. Prepare the recipe as directed, replacing the egg noodles with the drained rice noodles and reducing the added water to 1/4 cup.

pork & shrimp with egg noodles & basil
Prepare the basic recipe, but substitute 8 ounces sliced pork fillet for the chicken.

vegetables & egg noodles (vegetable lo mein)

see base recipe page 258

chicken lo mein
Omit the carrot, yellow bell pepper, and green beans from the basic recipe. Complete
the recipe as directed, adding 1 pound thinly sliced skinless chicken fillet to the wok after
the mushrooms.

pork lo mein
Prepare the basic recipe, but substitute 1 pound thinly sliced pork fillet for the mushrooms.

beef lo mein
Prepare the basic recipe, but substitute 1 pound thinly sliced beef sirloin for the mushrooms.

shrimp lo mein
Prepare the basic recipe, but substitute 1 pound of peeled and deveined shrimp for the
mushrooms.

glossary

basil: There are many varieties of basil available in addition to the common sweet Mediterranean basil. Opal basil has large purple leaves and a gingery, sweet flavor; holy basil, or hot basil, has a hot and spicy taste similar to cloves; and Thai basil has a slightly aniseed or licorice taste and small green leaves that have purplish stems.

bean pastes and sauces: Used for thousands of years by the Chinese, bean pastes and sauces are made from fermented and salted yellow and black soybeans. They have a very pungent aroma and are used as a seasoning for stir-fries and other foods; some also include chile and other seasonings. Fermented black and yellow soybeans can also be purchased whole and used to create your own sauces.

brassicas: There are many varieties of cabbage and broccoli that belong to the brassica family and are used in Asian cooking.

bok choy is a mild flavored, open-leaved cabbage with fat white or pale green stems and dark green leaves. Also known as bak choy, Chinese chard, Chinese white cabbage, and pak choy.

chinese broccoli is similar to western-style broccoli but has smaller florets on longer stems, coarse leaves, and a slightly bitter taste. It comes in green and dark purple varieties. The stems are used along with the leaves and florets. Tougher, bigger stems need to be peeled. Also known as Chinese kale, gai larn, gai lum, and kanah.

chinese cabbage is a mild flavored, slightly sweet cabbage that is wonderfully versatile. It can be eaten raw or cooked. Chinese cabbage is elongated in shape and has pale green, crinkly leaves. Shred or roughly chop it for use in stir-fries, and add it toward the end of cooking, discarding the central core. Also known as celery cabbage, napa cabbage, Peking cabbage, petsai, wom bok, and wong bok.

chinese flowering cabbage is a mild mustard-flavored vegetable that has long pale green stems, smooth green leaves, and tiny clusters of flowers on the tips of the inner shoots. Also known as choy sum.

tatsoi is a type of bok choy that has shiny dark green leaves that grow out from the center like a giant flower. Also known as flat cabbage, rosette bok choy, and rosette cabbage.

chile: Chiles belong to the pepper family and originated in South and Central America. Chiles can be made into pastes, sauces, and oils; or used fresh, dried, or powdered. Chiles don't just vary in their degree of heat, they also have distinctive flavors and are used in specific ways. The heat of chiles varies considerably, even within the same variety. The most common chiles used for stir-frying are the long red and green chiles, which are quite mild, and bird's eye chiles, which are quite hot.

chili pastes: Used as condiments and seasonings for Asian dishes, chili pastes vary depending on their region of origin. Some are sweet, spicy, and sticky; others, such as sambal oelek, are hot, salty, and sour.

cilantro: This aromatic herb with bright green leaves has a pungent flavor. The stems and roots are used in Thai cooking, and the leaves may be added toward the end of cooking or as a garnish. The dried seeds (called coriander) are used to add a mild, lemony flavor.

coconut palm sugar: Made from the sap of palm trees and sold in an unrefined dark state, this is a soft sugar, though sometimes it is sold in solid cakes that can be grated or shaved for use. Use an equal amount of brown sugar if coconut palm sugar is unavailable.

curry pastes: Although curry pastes are intended to be the flavor base for curries, they can also be a great way to add extra flavor to stir-fries without a lot of preparation. They typically feature a combination of shrimp paste, chile, onion, garlic, lemongrass, galangal, and cilantro, along with other spices, that have been ground together to make a paste.

daikon: A member of the radish family, daikon has a firm, crisp, white flesh and a mild flavor, similar to a white turnip. Some varieties are more peppery in taste than others. Fresh daikon should be firm, smooth, and slightly shiny. Also known as Chinese radish, Japanese radish, mooli, and Oriental radish.

fish sauce: Made from salted, dried fish or shrimp that have been layered in barrels and left to ferment for three months, fish sauce is an amber to dark brown colored liquid that has a pungent, salty taste. If you cannot find fish sauce, add salt to taste.

fried shallots: Used as a condiment or sprinkled over cooked dishes, fried shallots are used to add flavor and crunch to savory dishes. They can be purchased in bags at Asian grocery stores.

galangal: A close relative to ginger, galangal is a rhizome (or root) with a hot, gingery-citrusy flavor; it is used in similar ways to garlic and ginger. It can be found in most Asian grocery stores.

garlic chives: Used as a vegetable, rather than as an herb, garlic chives either have a long, flat green leaf and taste strongly of garlic, or they have a yellow leaf and more mild flavor. Also known as Chinese garlic chives and Chinese chives.

hoisin sauce: A sweet, salty, and spicy red-brown sauce, hoisin sauce is Chinese in origin and made from fermented soybeans, onion, garlic, sugar, and spices. Along with being used as a sauce in stir-fry recipes, it can also be used as a marinade and for basting.

kaffir lime leaves: With a strong lime flavor, these dark green leaves are usually joined end to end in twos giving them a figure eight shape. They can be found fresh, frozen, and dried in Asian grocery stores and are used in a similar way to bay leaves. If using dried leaves, double the number the recipe calls for, because they are not as strongly flavored when dried.

kecap manis: A dark, sweet, thick soy sauce made from black soybeans. Also known as ketjap manis or sieu wan.

lemongrass: A tall, clumping grass that smells and tastes of lemon; the white lower part of lemongrass is used finely chopped, or the stems can be bruised and used in cooking and then removed before serving.

lotus root: The under-water rhizome (or root) of the lotus plant. It has a crisp, delicate flavor and a beautiful appearance; when sliced crossways, the internal holes of the root form a floral pattern. It is available fresh, frozen, dried, and canned from Asian grocery stores.

miso paste: Made from fermented soy beans, this paste and adds depth and flavor to dishes.

noodles: Noodles are easy to prepare and a great addition to any home pantry. They can be made with rice flour, wheat flour, mung bean starch, or potato starch, and they come in many different shapes, textures, and thicknesses.
  bean thread noodles: Made from mung bean starch, these thin noodles become transparent once cooked. Also known as cellophane, glass, or jelly noodles, or mung bean vermicelli.
  soba noodles: Made from buckwheat, or a mixture of wheat and buckwheat, soba noodles are a Japanese

noodle that have a firm texture once cooked and are pale brown in color with a slightly nutty taste.

egg noodles: Made from eggs and wheat flour, egg noodles are available in many different shapes.

hokkien noodles: Thick, round egg noodles that have been partly cooked, lightly oiled, and packaged.

ramen noodles: are egg noodles and are available fresh, dried, or as instant noodles.

rice noodles: Made from rice flour and water, some (such as rice sticks and vermicelli) are available dried and others (such as laksa) are available fresh.

udon noodles: Thick, white Japanese noodles made from wheat flour; found fresh, dried, and frozen.

wheat noodles: Thin, round noodles made from wheat flour, these can be found dried and fresh.

oil: An important ingredient in stir-frying, your choice of oil may change the flavor of the finished dish and will play a part in how hot you can heat your wok. Different oils have different smoke and combustion points. The best oils to use at the high heat required for stir-frying are peanut oil, vegetable oils (such as canola oil), coconut oil, grapeseed oil, and rice bran oil.

oyster sauce: A thick and richly flavored brown sauce that is made from dried oysters, brine, and soy sauce and that is thickened with starches. It adds flavor to cooked dishes and can be used as a condiment. A vegetarian version is available using mushrooms instead of oysters.

rice wine: Often used to add flavor in Asian cooking, a couple different types of rice wine are available. Shaoxing, which is a Chinese rice wine, and mirin, a Japanese rice wine, are found in Asian grocery stores, but can be substituted in equal quantities with dry white wine, dry sherry, or dry vermouth.

shrimp paste: Made from partially fermented shrimp that have been ground, salted, and dried, shrimp paste has a pungent, salty flavor and should be used very sparingly as a seasoning in Asian dishes.

szechuan peppercorns: Widely used in Chinese cooking, Szechuan peppercorns have a mildly peppery, woody, spicy smell and a numbing, tingling aftertaste. They come from the red berries of the prickly ash tree and are sold whole or ground. Also known as anise, Chinese aromatic, or Sichuan peppercorns, and xanthoxylan.

tamarind pulp: A sticky, fleshy pulp that has a slightly astringent, sweet-sour taste and comes from the pods of the tamarind tree, tamarind pulp is used to add a sour taste to food. It can be purchased as a concentrate or paste, or as a dried block that must be soaked and pressed through a strainer to separate the pulp from the seeds. If tamarind paste is not available, substitute with a mixture of equal parts sugar and lime juice.

tempeh: A food made from partially fermented soy beans.

vietnamese mint: With a pungent, peppery flavor, Vietnamese mint is slightly similar to cilantro in taste, but sharper. It is actually a member of the buckwheat family, rather than a true variety of mint.

water chestnut: Small, brown tubers with white, crisp flesh and a nutty taste, water chestnuts resemble their namesake in appearance. Sold fresh or canned, they are used for texture and crunch in Asian cooking, and are therefore usually added toward the end of cooking.

yardlong bean: A long, green, stringless bean that can grow up to 16 inches (40 cm.) long, yardlong beans are similar in flavor to other beans. Usually available fresh from Asian grocery stores; if not available, stringless green beans can be substituted. Also called snake beans.

index